D0644230

On-the-Job Prayers

On-the-Job Prayers

101 Reflections and Prayers
for Christians in Every Occupation

William David Thompson

acta
PUBLICATIONS

On-the-Job Prayers
101 Reflections and Prayers for Christians in Every Occupation
by William David Thompson

Edited by Marcia Broucek
Cover design by Tom A. Wright
Cover art by Paulo Schiraldi of Creazioni Artistiche
from the collection of Gregory F. A. Pierce
Text Design and typesetting by Patricia Lynch

All Scripture quotations are from the *New Revised Standard Version Bible*,
copyright © 1989 by the Division of Christian Education of the National Council
of the Churches of Christ in the USA. Used by permission.

Sources and permissions for the readings and prayers used in this book are listed
in Resources for Readers on page 103. This should be considered a continuation of
this credit page.

Copyright © 2006 by William David Thompson

Published by:
ACTA Publications
Assisting Christians To Act
5559 W. Howard Street
Skokie, IL 60077
800-397-2282
www.actapublications.com

Library of Congress Number: 2005937148
ISBN 10: 0-87946-302-3
ISBN 13: 978-0-87946-302-1
Printed in Canada
Year: 15 14 13 12 10 9 8 7 6
Printing: 10 9 8 7 6 5 4 3 2 1

Contents

In memory of
Kirk, Rebecca, Audrey and Sander

A Word from the Publisher

*P*rayer at work is a tricky thing. On the one hand, we don't want to fall into the trap of the Pharisees and try to show others in our workplaces just how holy we are. We've all seen enough of that.

But on the other hand, in the midst of the hustle and bustle of our work, we need to remind ourselves that God is, indeed, present and we'd better take note and act accordingly. Humans have always turned to prayer to accomplish that task, and the workplace is no different from anyplace else.

So we have to figure out ways to raise our awareness of the divine presence on our jobs—without either offending or disturbing our fellow workers or disrupting the flow of the work itself, because the work is holy and needs to be done and our colleagues deserve to have their beliefs (or lack thereof) respected.

That is why we are delighted to be publishing Bill Thompson's wonderful book, *On-the-Job Prayers*. This is the workplace prayer book that many of us have been searching for: concise, practical, insightful, effective and efficient. The Scripture quote sets us up for a short reflection from the growing literature on the spirituality of work, and then we pray a short prayer written by Bill (marked WDT) or chosen by him. If we have a particular issue that we are dealing with, we can find a reflection and prayer on that subject in the Subject Index. Or we can just graze through the book as the Spirit moves us. And if we want to dig deeper into the connection between our faith and our work, we can read one of the books or search for more prayers or visit one of the websites in the Resources for Readers section.

Then a few minutes later we're back to work with a renewed awareness that our work and how we do it has real meaning in the big scheme of things; a renewed attitude toward our employees, bosses, colleagues, customers, clients, suppliers and competitors; and a renewed commitment to balance our work with the other important aspects of our life, including family and friends, church and community. Our work still gets done, we feel a little more fulfilled and at peace, and our fellow workers might even wonder what is in that little book we keep hidden in our lunchpail or briefcase or desk drawer.

So enjoy *On-the-Job Prayers*. You might even want to write a few prayers of your own and send them to us (at spiritualitywork@aol.com) for the inevitable sequel. Meanwhile, thank you for all the good work that you do every day.

Gregory F. Augustine Pierce
President and Co-Publisher
ACTA Publications

Introduction

The workplace is where we spend the major part of our lives—in both time and energy. We put things together and we create new ideas; we buy and we sell; we make new products and we fix what gets broken; we advise and we heal; we teach and we manage; we compete and we build relationships. In other words, we do what it takes to make the world function. While homemakers are not on a payroll, they, too, work to make the family function— and thus the world. Is it any wonder that the big dictionaries print a dazzling variety of meanings for the word *work?* Someone has defined work as "hell with fluorescent lights." Many people would agree, because their life at work is unsatisfying, even painful. Making it through the day is tough for many people, while others love their work, at least most of the time. But we all need to draw on God's help for the situations that challenge us.

This book is based on the idea that spirituality of work is just as important as any other kind of spirituality—of contemplative prayer, of nature, or of a highly developed religious system. Teachers of contemplative prayer speak of that experience as a "thin place," enabling an intimacy between the person praying and God. In contrast, the workplace seems to most of us as a "thick place" where God does not seem so accessible. The reality is that God is everywhere, immediately available to listen to us, to forgive us, to encourage us, to empower us. We can experience God's presence at our desks, our labs, our kitchens, our classrooms, our stores, our factory floors, our hospital corridors, our street corners—wherever we make a living.

A number of wonderful books have been written recently on spirituality in the workplace. You can learn a lot from them. This book takes a different approach. Rather than telling you *about* spirituality, *On-the-Job Prayers* invites you to *practice* spirituality by going into the very presence of God for help on a topic that is illuminated by Scripture and informed by thoughtful reflection. You will learn about spirituality in the workplace experientially, not just intellectually. As you reflect and pray, you are making a significant spiritual journey.

On-the-Job Prayers is for people who go to work every day with the resources of the Christian faith: a belief in God who creates, in Jesus Christ who redeems, and in the Holy Spirit who guides. Each page contains a Scripture quote to direct your spirit toward God and focus on an important issue. Each quote is accompanied by a reading to help you think about the life of the Spirit in your workplace.

The readings draw on a variety of sources for inspiration and guidance: some written by well-known people, some from the books and articles about spirituality in the workplace, some passages from the Bible, and others from a variety of thinkers and writers. They deal with the issues that every Christian who tries to put Christian values into practice on the job faces, such as practicing the presence of God in the workplace, taking care of the earth, treating people with respect, making difficult career choices, and making decisions with integrity.

At the conclusion of each page is a workplace prayer to help you lift your concerns, both for yourself and for other workers, to God. Enter into each prayer fully, praying it silently or aloud as you wish and are able. You may want to begin the prayer by asking God to hear the written prayer as your own. You may choose to breathe a silent "Amen" or "Yes, Lord" as you read. You may want to pray for someone you love—or someone who is hard to love. You may wish to pray for a congregation or a cause about which you feel deeply. The important thing is that you make the prayer your own.

The prayers come from a variety of sources and traditions. Many of them were written especially for this book. Most are in contemporary language, but a few are in the beautiful cadences of seventeenth-century English with the occasional *thee* and *thou*. Some are in a conversational mode; others written in beautiful poetry. Most of the prayers are personal, using the pronouns *I* and *me*. Others are inclusive, using *us* and *ours*. When you pray in *we* and *us* language, you may be praying on behalf of your family, your faith community, or the people you work with—or all three.

Between the readings and the prayer—or after you have prayed—spend a few moments in silence to listen to what God is saying to you.

You may use *On-the-Job Prayers* at any time, but it is designed for the beginning of your workday. To get the greatest benefit, choose a specific time for this spiritual discipline. It may help to get to your workplace a few minutes before your day begins or set aside time before family activities distract you. Put this book on top of your "to do" list for the day, or at the top of a drawer you access to start the day, or anywhere in plain sight. If break time or the lunch hour works better for you, start that time with the reading of a page as a sacred moment: it will take you only a minute. Another way to optimize this experience is to claim for yourself a single word or short phrase from the Scripture, reading or prayer. Let it seep into your consciousness so it is available to you throughout the day when you need God's presence or power.

On-the-Job Prayers has been prepared in the hope and expectation that, with or without fluorescent lights, your workplace, enriched by your daily prayers, will become a little more like heaven.

William David Thompson
Drexal Hill, Pennsylvania

101 Reflections and Prayers
for Christians in Every Occupation

Hidden Saints

It is a timely coincidence that Christianity is seeking to be more relevant to the world of business when at the same time the American marketplace desires to reassess the meaning of work. At the same time that U.S. society is interested in humanizing the workplace in order to stay competitive and productive, the Christian community is struggling with its desire to upgrade the worldly life of its hidden saints—people at work in the world. Both America and Christianity are now beginning to recognize that work is a fundamental dimension of human existence and that work is a key to the values of the human enterprise.

—William Droel, *The Spirituality of Work*

WORKPLACE PRAYER

Merciful God, I've never thought of myself as a hidden saint—or any other kind of saint, for that matter. But I understand that, as a Christian, I have something distinctive to contribute to my workplace. Help me to model integrity, respect for all kinds of people, and a life-work balance. Help me to connect my faith with what people see of me and my work. Strengthen my sense that my work is a calling from you. Amen.

—WDT

Lead a life worthy of the calling to which you have been called, with all humility and gentleness, with patience, bearing with one another in love.

—*Ephesians 4:1b-2*

*For what will it
profit them to gain
the whole world and
forfeit their life?*

—Mark 8:36

What Is a Job?

Jobs are what people do for a living, many of them for eight hours a day, five days a week, minus vacations, for most of their lives. It is tragic to think how few of them have their hearts in it. They work mainly for the purpose of making money enough to enjoy their moments of not working. If not working is the chief pleasure they have, you wonder if they wouldn't do better just to devote themselves to that from the start. They would probably end up in breadlines or begging, but, even so, the chances are that they would be happier than they would be pulling down a good salary as a bank teller or a dental technician or a supermarket bagger and hating every minute of it.

"What do people gain from all the toil at which they toil under the sun?" asks the Preacher (Ecclesiastes 1:3). If people are in it only for the money, the money is all they gain, and when they finally retire, they may well ask themselves if it was worth giving most of their lives for. If they're doing it for its own sake—if they enjoy doing it and the world needs it done—it may very possibly help to gain them their own souls.

—Frederick Buechner, *Beyond Words*

WORKPLACE PRAYER

God of My Heart, you know my thoughts about my job today. You know the things that bore me, that frustrate me, that challenge me, that delight me. Help me to see your deeper purpose. I pray today especially for the people in my workplace whose jobs seem meaningless to them—and for the times when my own work seems to lack purpose. I pray for those whose jobs are humdrum, monotonous or poorly paid. Give hope to those who can only see themselves spending their working lives at the bottom of the ladder. Remind me that you value every worker I will encounter today. Give me your heart for what I do and your joy in the doing. Amen.

—WDT

Escaping the Rat Race

"The problem with the rat race is that even if you win, you're still a rat," jokes comedienne Lily Tomlin. And the problem with being a rat at work is that it tends to make your home into a rat hole. Work is an important element of family life, whether it is paid work outside or inside the home, unpaid work at home, or volunteer work at church or in community or civic organizations. If our work is viewed as a necessary evil, a burden to be borne, a "daily grind," then it cannot help but have a negative impact on family life. If mother or father and/or children detest the work, view it as something that detracts from family life, and complain about it all the time, then this attitude is going to permeate family life as well. Conversely, if family members are workaholics or consider their work as the really important part of life, then this too can destroy family life. On the other hand, if work is spiritual, that is, if it is conducted in a balanced manner in line with our deepest convictions and values, then work itself can provide the foundation and even enhance the spirituality of family life.

—Gregory F. A. Pierce, *Spirituality at Work*

Do not work for the food that perishes, but for the food that endures for eternal life, which the Son of Man will give you. For it is on him that God the Father has set his seal.

—John 6:27

WORKPLACE PRAYER

Giver and Sustainer, you know how hard it is to strike a balance between the time and energy I give to my work and what I seem to have left to give to my family and friends. I need your help to acknowledge the limits of my physical, emotional and spiritual resources, and to use them well in both places. Help me to be aware of your presence and power in my work life and in my life beyond the job. You are the one God, and I am one person made in your image. By your Spirit show me how to experience the wholeness of life lived by your Spirit, lived in your love. May my whole life be sustained by you and used by you to make the world a better place. Amen.

—WDT

I keep the Lord always before me; because he is at my right hand, I shall not be moved. Therefore my heart is glad, and my soul rejoices; my body also rests secure.... You show me the path of life. In your presence there is fullness of joy; in your right hand are pleasures forevermore.

—Psalm 16:8-9,11

A Calming Presence

May you trust God that you are exactly where you are meant to be.
May you not forget the infinite possibilities that are born of faith.
May you use the gifts that you have received
    and pass on the greatest of those gifts
      —the love that has been given to you.
May you be content, knowing that you are a child of God,
God be in your sitting down, your rising up, your coming and your
    going.
Let God's presence settle into your bones,
    and cherish the freedom to praise God
    with your lips, your life, and especially your work.
Above all, may God give you the openness to hear his voice
    and to become his presence
    in that place to which you have been called.

—Author unknown

WORKPLACE PRAYER

O God, the unseen but real presence in this world, you are here in my place of work just as surely as I am. Thank you for your promise to be with me always. Help me to become increasingly aware that, in the midst of all that goes on here, I am not alone, nor am I ever lacking the love you provide so freely. Let your presence settle into my bones, your joy in my body, your love in my heart. Today and every day may I become your loving presence to those with whom I work. Amen.

—Author unknown

The Workers' Twenty-Third Psalm

The Lord is my real boss, and I shall not want.

He gives me peace when chaos is all around me.

He gently reminds me to pray and do all things without murmuring and complaining.

He reminds me that he is my source (and not my job).

He restores my sanity every day and guides my decisions that I might honor him in all that I do.

Even though I face an absurd amount of e-mails, system crashes, unrealistic deadlines, budget cutbacks, gossiping co-workers, discriminating supervisors and an aging body that doesn't cooperate every morning, I still will not stop, for he is with me!

His presence, his peace, and his power will see me through.

He raises me up, even when they fail to promote me.

He claims me as his own, even when the company threatens to let me go.

His faithfulness and love are better than any bonus check.

His retirement plan beats every 401k there is!

When it's all said and done, I'll be working for him a whole lot longer.

And for that, I bless his name!

—Author unknown

WORKPLACE PRAYER

God, you are my Comforter. I am grateful that your peace is greater than all the chaos around me. You know what I face at work today; you know how much I have to do. And you promise to be with me in every discussion, decision and difficult task. Just as you claim me, so I claim your faithfulness and love. Walk with me throughout this day and restore my soul. Amen.

—WDT

On-the-Job Prayer

5

The Lord is my shepherd, I shall not want. He makes me lie down in green pastures; he leads me beside still waters; he restores my soul. He leads me in right paths for his name's sake.

—Psalm 23:1-3

Therefore, my beloved, be steadfast, immovable, always excelling in the work of the Lord, because you know that in the Lord your labor is not in vain.

—1 Corinthians 15:58

Work as a Path to Holiness

In many religious traditions, work is not set off from the precincts of the sacred. It is not "pro-fane"—in front of the temple—it *is* the temple. In Christian and Zen monasteries, for instance, work is as much a part of the monk's carefully designed life as are prayer, meditation, and liturgy. I learned this when I was a novice in a religious order. A novice is a fledgling monk, learning the ins and outs of the spiritual life of prayer, meditation, study and…work. I recall one day in particular when I was given the job of pruning apple trees. It was a cold day in Wisconsin, and I was out on a limb sawing away at shoots sticking up on limbs all around me like minarets. I took a minute to rest, hoping the limb wouldn't suddenly break, and asked myself, "Why am I doing this? I'm supposed to be learning prayer, meditation, Latin and Gregorian chant. But here I am, my hands frostbitten, feeling not terribly secure in the top of a tree, my fingers bloody from an erratic saw blade, doing something I know nothing about." The answer, I already knew, was that work is an important component of the spiritual life. In some monasteries, monks file off to work in procession, wearing their long hooded robes and maintaining silence. Monastic writers describe work as a path to holiness.

—Thomas Moore, *Care of the Soul*

✦

WORKPLACE PRAYER

Work is your gift to us, a call to reach new heights for the good of all. Guide us as we work and teach us to live in the spirit that has made us your sons and daughters, in the love that has made us brothers and sisters. Amen.

—William Byron, SJ

Making a Difference

Happiness requires an investment of one's inner world in something bigger—the outer world—and it brings with it a sense of self-worth and self-value. When I believe I have made a difference to some person by my time, talent, or energy, or when I believe I have created something new in the world that could benefit someone, I believe that my life really matters, that it does make a difference to this bigger reality. In some small way, I have made the world a better place. I have made a net positive difference by my existence. My life, my existence, my talents, and my energies are objectively significant. The objective world around me is better because of my presence, and I know it. This sense of objective significance makes me feel more alive, more at home in the universe, exhilarated. It awakens my spirit. I feel connected to what is beyond my inner world through the positivity that I contribute to it.

—Robert Spitzer, *The Spirit of Leadership*

WORKPLACE PRAYER

Eternal Friend, you know that my heart and mind are filled with how much needs to get done today. Help me to refocus on your larger reality, on the things that really matter. Help me use my energy wisely and effectively today to make a difference among my co-workers, my family, my friends. Help me to speak on your behalf, to extend your grace in the world. Help me to be a good steward of the gifts you have given me so I can help, in some small way, to make the world a better place. Most of all, keep me connected with your vision of grace for this busy, changing world. Amen.

—WDT

Just as we have the same spirit of faith that is in accordance with scripture—"I believed, and so I spoke"—we also believe, and so we speak…so that grace, as it extends to more and more people, may increase thanksgiving, to the glory of God.

—2 Corinthians 4:13, 15

On-the-Job Prayer

8

Speaking the truth in love, we must grow up in every way into him who is the head, into Christ, from whom the whole body, joined and knit together by every ligament with which it is equipped, as each part is working properly, promotes the body's growth in building itself up in love.

—Ephesians 4:15-16

What We Are About

Wherever we work, we need courage both to remember what we are about and, according to the tenor of our times, reimagine ourselves while we are doing it. We are not alone in this endeavor but secretly pointed to all those who struggle out loud where we have not yet begun to speak, or when we are loud and vociferous, to those who labor painfully and secretly beside us. We are joined especially with those now silent who have come before us. We represent not only ourselves but those who have gifted us the possibilities of the present. In the satisfaction of good work is not only the fulfillment of a very personal dream but the harvest of generations of hope and toil.

—David Whyte, *Crossing the Unknown Sea: Work as a Pilgrimage of Identity*

WORKPLACE PRAYER

Loving God, you made us co-creators in the process of your creation, blessing us with wisdom, reason, creativity, and skill. Bless all who seek meaningful employment that they may provide for the well-being of their families. Let those who have more than they need for life's necessities be moved to use their wealth to create new opportunities for others. Let those who have skills be open to sharing the riches of their knowledge with those who seek the opportunity to learn. Let us all learn from one another, for you have blessed every human being with a gift for the benefit of the common good. And thereby enable us by the power of your Holy Spirit to build up the body of Christ on this earth that your name be proclaimed and blessed through the good work of all. In Christ's name we pray. Amen.

—Vienna Cobb Anderson, *Prayers of Our Hearts in Word and Action*

Trusting God's Presence

Over the past four years I have spent a considerable proportion of my time listening to people in their workplace talking about their daily pressures and responsibilities. Most, but not all, of these people are active Christians who want to integrate their faith with their work in a practical and consistent manner. The single, most commonly expressed priority has been how to practise the presence of God at work. Many Christians have a discipline of personal prayer and Bible study, usually on a daily basis—however brief or interrupted. Most are involved in public worship on Sundays in their local churches. A few try to attend a lunchtime service in one of the city churches during the week. All these opportunities add up to a personal spirituality of considerable significance. All would agree in principle to the truth that God is present with them in their work. From time to time, perhaps during a crisis or in a rare slack period, they make the opportunity to practice God's presence—to pray about their work, their colleagues, their pressures. But it is rare.

—David Prior, "Practicing God's Presence at Work," *Faith at Work*

Our soul waits for the Lord; he is our help and shield. Our heart is glad in him, because we trust in his holy name. Let your steadfast love, O Lord, be upon us, even as we hope in you.

—Psalm 33:20-22

WORKPLACE PRAYER

Help me, God, when the going gets rough, to trust in you for help. You know the pressures I face at work today. I need to know that I am not alone in my struggles, that you are always with me. You have sustained people in troubles far more serious than my own, and I trust you to give me a sense of your presence and your power in the work I have before me today. Thank you for your promise of steadfast love. My hope is in you. Amen.

—WDT

On-the-Job Prayer

10

This is the day that the Lord has made; let us rejoice and be glad in it.

—Psalm 118:24

Today Is Precious

Today. It is a moment of light surrounded on all sides by darkness and oblivion. In the entire history of the universe, let alone in your own history, there has never been another just like it and there will never be another just like it again. It is the point to which all your yesterdays have been leading since the hour of your birth. It is the point from which all your tomorrows will proceed until the hour of your death. If you were aware of how precious it is, you could hardly live through it. Unless you are aware of how precious it is, you can hardly be said to be living at all…. The point is to see it for what it is, because it will be gone before you know it. If you waste it, it is your life that you're wasting. If you look the other way, it may be the moment you've been waiting for always that you're missing. All other days have either disappeared into darkness and oblivion or not yet emerged from it. Today is the only day there is.

—Frederick Buechner, *Beyond Word*

WORKPLACE PRAYER

O God,
Give me the strength to live another day;
Let me not turn coward before its difficulties;
Let me not lose faith in other people;
Keep me sweet and sound of heart,
    in spite of ingratitude, treachery or meanness…
Preserve me from minding little stings or giving them;
Help me to keep my heart clean
    and to live so honestly and fearlessly
      that no outward failure can dishearten me
      or take away the joy of conscious integrity;
Open wide the eyes of my soul that I may see good in all things;
Grant me this day a new vision of your truth;
Inspire me with the spirit of joy and gladness;
    whatever this day of work brings forth;
In the name of the strong deliverer,
    our only Lord and Savior, Jesus Christ. Amen.

—Phillips Brooks (1835-1893)

The Spirituality of Work

It seems that "spirituality of work" is an oxymoron: two ideas that at first do not seem to go together, like "jumbo shrimp" or "tough love." I'm going to assume that there is a spirituality of work that can be every bit as rich, satisfying, challenging, and compelling as the most traditional monastic or mystical spirituality. In the Buddhist tradition there is a story of a woman who finally became enlightened. When she was asked what the difference was, she described it this way: "Before I was enlightened, I chopped wood and I hauled water. After I was enlightened, I chopped wood and I hauled water." I think that the spirituality of work is much like this. We can be doing exactly the same work before we begin practicing the spirituality of work as we do afterward. But both our spirituality and our work are changed by the very act of making the connection.

—Gregory F. A. Pierce, *Spirituality at Work*

WORKPLACE PRAYER

O God, I know that my faith is supposed to affect the whole of my life—my relationships, my job, my time. But I have trouble making the connection in every situation, especially in the tough times at work. Help me to be open to your Spirit today so that both the quality of my faith and the quality of my work grow together. Amen.

—WDT

If anyone is in Christ, there is a new creation: everything old has passed away; see, everything has become new!

—2 Corinthians 5:17

*Show yourself in all
respects a model of
good works, and in
your teaching show
integrity, gravity, and
sound speech that
cannot be censured.*

—*Titus 2:7-8*

Good Work

In every historical era, many people have sought to carry out good work. It has always been true that some people do their work expertly but not very responsibly. People who do good work, in our sense of the term, are clearly skilled in one or more professional realms. At the same time, rather than merely following money or fame alone, of choosing the path of least resistance when in conflict, they are thoughtful about their responsibilities and the implications of their work. At best, they are concerned to act in a responsible fashion with respect toward their personal goals; their family, friends, peers and colleagues; their mission of sense of calling; the institutions with which they are affiliated; and lastly, the wider world—people they do not know, those who will come afterwards, and, in the grandest sense, to the planet or to God.

—Howard Gardner, Mihaly Csikszentmihalyi
and William Damon, *Good Work*

WORKPLACE PRAYER

Merciful God, forgive me when I fail to be thoughtful about the responsibilities and implications of my work. At some level I understand that my work is an integral part of the work of the world, but very often I'm so involved in the daily details that I don't see the larger picture. As a Christian, I affirm that I am responsible to you for the quality of my work—more responsible to you, indeed, than I am to those who manage me. Keep me focused today, I pray, on the highest sense of "good work"—namely work that pleases you. Amen.

—WDT

What Is Success?

What is your image of a successful person? More often than not, it is probably a Type A personality. A "successful" person is usually aggressive, hard driving, always moving, the first in the office in the morning and the last to leave at night. Often he or she is consumed by a frantic kind of busyness and motivated by strong forces to get ahead. An inability to be a Type A person doesn't constitute failure in God's economy. God wants you to be consumed by him, not by your work. The way to success is not a corporate ladder. Rather it is through a relationship with Christ. In that relationship God wants us to live his way of life, his commands integrated into our daily activities.

—Richard Malone, *Devotions for Job Seekers*

WORKPLACE PRAYER

O Lord, grant that my heart may be truly cleansed and filled with the Holy Spirit, and that I may arise to serve thee, and lie down to sleep in entire confidence in thee, and in submission to thy will, ready for life or for death. Let me live for the day, not overcharged with worldly cares, but feeling that my treasure is not here, and desiring truly to be joined to thee in thy heavenly kingdom. O Lord, save me from sin and guide me with thy spirit and keep me in faithful obedience to thee, through Jesus Christ thy Son, our Lord. Amen.

—Thomas Arnold (1795-1842)

On-the-Job Prayer

13

Strive first for the kingdom of God and his righteousness, and all these things will be given to you as well.

—*Matthew 6:33*

---

*Do your best to
present yourself to
God as one approved
by him, a worker
who has no need to be
ashamed.*

—*2 Timothy 2:15*

Always Care

Success in life has been described as the maintained ecstasy of burning with a hard, gemlike flame. The image recurs. In his famous essay on Ted Williams's final game, "Hub Fans Bid Kid Adieu," John Updike wrote of Williams radiating "the hard blue glow of high purpose." Updike said, "For me, Williams is the classic ballplayer of the game on a hot August weekday before a small crowd, when the only thing at stake is the tissue-thin difference between a thing done well and a thing done ill." Baseball, played on a field thinly populated with men rhythmically shifting from languor to tension, is, to Updike's eyes, an essentially lonely game. The cool mathematics of individual performances are the pigments coloring the long season of averaging out. Baseball heroism comes not from flashes of brilliance but rather, Updike says, "from the players who always care" about themselves and their craft.

—George F. Will, *Men at Work*

WORKPLACE PRAYER

O God, I know what it feels like to be a lonely player at work. There are others, of course, or we could not get the work done. But sometimes it seems that I am the only one doing all the work, and sometimes it is a lonely game. I know when I am doing well, and more acutely, when I am doing less than I am capable of doing. I know that what all of us do will somehow average out so that we can make this enterprise a success. Where I need help today is in seeing the dynamic relationship between myself and everyone else. Mostly, I need to care deeply about my work. Forgive me when I don't and help me to do my best in the work you have given me to do. Amen.

—WDT

The Wealth of Creativity

The philosopher Alfred North Whitehead once remarked that the rise of modern science was inconceivable apart from the habits human beings learned during long centuries of tutelage under Judaism and Christianity. Judaism and Christianity taught humans that the whole world and everything in it are intelligible, because all things—even contingent and seemingly accidental events—spring from the mind of an all-knowing Creator. This teaching had great consequences in the practical order. Man the discoverer is made in the image of God. To be creative, to cooperate in bringing creation itself to its perfection is an important element of the human vocation. The belief that each human being is *imago deo*—made in the image of God—was bound to lead, in an evolutionary and experimental way, to the development of an economic system whose first premise is that the principal cause of wealth is human creativity.

—Michael Novak, *Business as a Calling*

WORKPLACE PRAYER

Giver of All Things, I don't very often think of wealth and possessions as having much to do with you. Yet the human creativity that develops our economic system is part of your gift to the world. Human imagination is a reflection of you. Thank you that I am made in your image—with personality, the ability to make choices and the desire to create. Help me to use those gifts well as I work today. I need to acknowledge you, O God, as the all-knowing Creator. And I need to place the accumulation of money in its proper place. Let me not put devotion to money above my devotion to you. Help me to trust you to meet my needs, and give me the good sense to use responsibly what you provide. Amen.

—WDT

For the love of money is a root of all kinds of evil, and in their eagerness to be rich some have wandered away from the faith and pierced themselves with many pains. But as for you...shun all this; pursue righteousness, godliness, faith, love, endurance, gentleness.

—1 Timothy 6:10-11

---

*Be doers of the word,
and not merely
hearers…those who
look into the perfect
law, the law of liberty,
and persevere, being
not hearers who forget
but doers who act—
they will be blessed in
their doing.*

—James 1:22, 25

It's Time to Act

The world needs your creativity. Now is the time for you to make your original contributions. No longer is it appropriate to sit back and let others do everything. The national and global crises we face today demand that each of us do what we can. No matter how small your action may appear, it will have an effect, so don't hold back. Your experience and wisdom is important as a piece of the overall tapestry. Everything is changing. The fields of health, education, communications, politics, science, travel, social service, media, and finance are undergoing dramatic transformation in countless ways. We're living in the midst of an exciting, exhilarating and challenging time, ripe for seminal change at many levels. The father of modern psychology, William James, once set himself the dictum, "I will act as if what I do makes a difference." Not only did he change his own life, he affected the lives of millions of others, and his legacy continues long after his death. You'll never know the full power and effect of your actions. But it's crucial that you act.

—Michael and Justine Willis Toms, *True Work*

WORKPLACE PRAYER

For all who work to help make the world function, I pray.
For the unemployed and those who work without a living wage,
    I pray.
For families unable to support themselves, I pray.
For those unable to work, I pray.
For those whose livelihood is threatened by technology, I pray.
For persons whose families suffer because of workplace pressures,
    I pray.
For persons with decision making power but without a moral
    compass, I pray.
For myself I pray that I may act in these challenging times with
    your power.
Lord, grant your grace to all of us, that your will may be done in the
    workplace.
Amen.

—Author unknown

Human Capital

If you were to ask a group of enlightened CEO's to tell you the two most critical issues for business in the next century they would answer, "How to tap the deepest levels of creativity and the highest levels of productivity of our employees." In a world where competition has become global and where knowledge and technology flow readily across international boundaries, companies are learning that the only way to build real competitive advantage is through their human capital. This is forcing companies to take a hard look at their corporate cultures and values. Enlightened leaders are learning that employee fulfillment, environmental stewardship, and social responsibility will be the keys to increased productivity and creativity in the future. The values that corporations hold are increasingly affecting their ability to hire the best people and sell their products.

—Richard Barrett, *Liberating the Corporate Soul*

WORKPLACE PRAYER

Lord of the universe, we praise you for your creation, for the wonders of space, the beauty of the world, the value of the earth's resources, and the skills of hand and brain which enrich our lives. We thank you for humanity in all its diversity, for the unique individuality of every child, woman and man, for the gathered communities of home, work and leisure, of village, city and nation. We thank you offering us the chance to share in creation through the work of hand and brain, for the opportunity to plan and design, to manufacture and grow, to serve and conserve, and to care for one another in the places where we work. We thank you for giving us special gifts and responsibilities, for enabling us to stand upright and make choices, for presenting us with opportunities to promote justice and truth. And because he shared with us our humanity and our world, we thank you for the gift of your Son Jesus Christ, our beginning and our end, who carried out your work to your praise and glory and for the renewal of your creation. So we make our prayer to you in his name, who died and rose again for us. Amen.

—*Faith in Business*

According to the grace of God given to me, like a skilled master builder I laid a foundation, and someone else is building on it. Each builder must choose with care how to build on it.

—*1 Corinthians 3:10*

On-the-Job Prayer

18

What matters is faith working through love.

—*Galatians 5:6b*

The Soul of the Community

Pressures of immediate tasks and the bottom line often crowd out personal needs that people bring into the workplace. Every organization is a family, whether caring or dysfunctional. Caring begins with knowing about others—it requires listening, understanding and accepting. It progresses through a deepening sense of appreciation, respect, and ultimately, love. Love is a willingness to reach out and open one's heart. An open heart is vulnerable. Accepting vulnerability allows us to drop our masks, meet heart to heart, and be present for one another. We experience a sense of unity and delight in voluntary, human exchanges that mold "the soul of the community."

—Lee G. Bolman and Terrence E. Deal, *Leading with Soul*

WORKPLACE PRAYER

Creator, how wonderfully you have fashioned the world. You have flung into space all the stars and the planets—galaxies without end. You have created the universe in an intricate and purposeful design. You have also fashioned the systems of the world, involving tens of millions of people in the making and distribution of goods and services that sustain its people. I give you thanks for the work you have given me to do. Enable me to see what I do not just as a job, but as a part of your grand design. Give me a new sense of caring about my co-workers today. Grant the people I work with a sense of community—a spirit of honesty, unselfishness, cooperation, faithfulness and joy—even love for each other. I offer this prayer and my work to you, O God, in the name of Jesus, who labored in the carpenter's shop and gave his life for us all. Amen.

—WDT

Using Your Resources

Indeed, besides the earth, man's principal resource is man himself. His intelligence enables him to discover the earth's productive potential and the many different ways which human needs can be satisfied. It is his disciplined work in close collaboration with others that makes possible the creation of ever more extensive working communities which can be relied upon to transform man's natural and human environments. Important virtues are involved in this process, such as diligence, industriousness, prudence in undertaking reasonable risks, reliability and fidelity in interpersonal relationships, as well as courage in carrying out decisions which are difficult and painful but necessary, both for the overall working of a business and in meeting possible setbacks.

—Pope John Paul II

WORKPLACE PRAYER

Provider and Sustainer, I am grateful for the work you have given me to do. Help me to use my intelligence and skills to be a productive contributor. Help me today to be especially aware of my part in the larger human community. I am grateful for those who use the services and products of the work we do here—customers, clients and vendors. Enable me to be sensitive to their needs and flexible in adapting to their changing situations. Sustain my commitment to do what is needed and give me the courage to move beyond indifference. May I do my part to make your transformation of the world possible. Amen.

—WDT

On-the-Job Prayer

19

Whatever your task, put yourselves into it.

—*Colossians 3:23*

How are they to call on one in whom they have not believed? And how are they to believe in one of whom they have never heard? And how are they to hear without someone to proclaim him? And how are they to proclaim him unless they are sent? As it is written, "How beautiful are the feet of those who bring good news!"

—*Romans 10:14-15*

Spiritual Hunger

It is commonplace to say that we are living in an age of spiritual hunger. I don't think there is a place in the world, certainly not in Western civilization, where that ravenous hunger is as intense and profound as it is in the workplace—the quest for meaning and significance in what we spend most of our waking hours doing. Faith in Christ is not merely church-house faith. It is faith all the time, everywhere, in everything—faith in all our places, all our houses, all our work. Not only do we need to understand that the word *church* refers first and foremost to people, not to buildings, but we also need to expand the meaning of the word itself to include something far beyond the local institutional church. Of course, congregational life is crucial, but the depth and vitality of congregational life is intended to give itself away in all the secular institutions of society through those of us who are its lay people. That is the only way the world can be changed. In our emphasis on the gathered church, the tragedy of our history is that we have neglected teaching the scattered church.

—Howard E. Butt, Jr., in *LayNet*

WORKPLACE PRAYER

Lord, I know that Christ has no body on earth but ours, no hands but ours, no feet but ours; ours are the eyes through which Christ looks out in compassion to the world, ours are the feet with which he is to go about doing good, and ours are the hands with which he is to bless the world now. Lord, make it so in my life, now and always. Amen.

—St. Teresa of Avila (1515-1582)

God's Hands and Feet

We believe that God is creating
in the clay of a potter
in the music of an orchestra,
in the bread of a baker.
We believe that Jesus Christ is present
in the hospitality of a waitress,
in the care of a social worker,
in the voice of a teacher.
We believe that the Holy Spirit is moving
in the healing touch of a doctor,
in the actions of a peacemaker,
in the laughter of a child.

—*Worship & Daily Life*

WORKPLACE PRAYER

Creator, Redeemer and Guide, help me today to be especially aware that I am your hands and feet in this world, that my actions can reflect your love and care. I want to affirm that my work is somehow not only mine but yours. Thank you that you have made humankind in your image, with the amazing ability to create. Help me honor those who make the world a more beautiful place by painting, singing, designing, building and cooking. Thank you for those to whom you have entrusted the work of fixing what is inefficient or broken, of sealing leaks in pipes, of repairing machinery, of making computers function at their best. Thank you for those to whom you have given the gift of helping as teachers, consultants, peacemakers, doctors. Give to all of us a sense that what we are doing is what you are doing through us to make the world work. Amen.

—WDT

On-the-Job Prayer

21

Ever since the creation of the world his eternal power and divine nature, invisible though they are, have been understood and seen through the things he has made.

—*Romans 1:20*

⬥

*So God created
humankind in his
image, in the image of
God he created them;
male and female he
created them. God
blessed them, and
God said to them,
"Be fruitful and
multiply, and fill the
earth and subdue it;
and have dominion
over the fish of the
sea and over the birds
of the air and over
every living thing
that moves upon the
earth."*

—Genesis 1:27-28

Improving the World

Someone has said that when God made the earth he could have finished it, but he didn't. He left it as raw material to set us thinking and experimenting, risking and adventuring. Thus we find our supreme interest in living. Notice that often children will ignore clever mechanical toys and build with spools, string, sticks and blocks, using the world of their own imagination. It's also true with adults. God gave us a world unfinished, that we might share in the joy and satisfaction of creation. He left electricity to be discovered in the clouds, bridges to be built, laboratories to be opened, diamonds to be cut, music, poetry, dramas to be written, sung and acted, children and adults to be taught. He gave us the challenge of uncountable raw materials, not the satisfaction of a perfectly finished world. With God's wisdom we can find all kinds of ways to improve our world and, believe it or not, our workplaces too.

—Dawn Elliott Davis, Ph.D., Educator

⬥

WORKPLACE PRAYER

Lord, I thank you for the challenges in life. I am grateful for the stimulating, exciting, creative activities that keep me thinking, working, experimenting and experiencing all the joys of achievement. I thank you for life itself and the strength to work earnestly toward important goals. Bless me today, I pray, and all who work here that we make creative use of what you give us of your creation. Amen.

—Dawn Elliott Davis

God in the Midst

Holiness is not limited to the sanctuary or to moments of private prayer; it is a call to direct our whole heart and life toward God and according to God's plan for the world. For the laity holiness is achieved in the midst of the world, in family, in community, in friendships, in work, in leisure, in citizenship.

We need a spirituality that calls forth and supports by initiative and witness not just in our churches but also in business, in the labor movement, in the professions, in education, and in public life. Our faith is not just a weekend obligation, a mystery to be celebrated around the altar on Sunday. It is a pervasive reality to be practiced everyday in homes, offices, factories, schools, and businesses across our land.

—U.S. Catholic Bishops, "Economic Justice for All"

WORKPLACE PRAYER

Eternal God, I know that your Spirit is present everywhere. You do not limit your presence and your power to a time and a place. You make yourself known wherever there is openness to you—even in this workplace and even to me. So give me, I pray, an awareness of you throughout this day. May my whole heart, and all the work of my mind and hands and feet, combine to bring your loving, creative and redemptive Spirit into this workplace. Amen.

—WDT

Where can I go from your spirit? Or where can I flee from your presence? If I take the wings of the morning and settle at the farthest limits of the sea, even there your hand shall lead me, and your right hand shall hold me fast.

—Psalm 139:7, 9-10

*For we are God's
servants, working
together; you are
God's field, God's
building.*

—*1 Corinthians 3:9*

God at Work

We know, when we stop to think, that we are dependent on industry, and yet we are unable to affirm industrial life as being of real worth. This is a basic sickness at the heart of our society, a failure in our fundamental attitudes. Put in religious terms, we are unable to relate our belief in the creative power and purpose of God to the existence of factories and mills and power stations and office blocks. In an agricultural society, praise is given to God for his power in the rhythm of seed-time and harvest, for his mercy in the fresh growth of grain and crops. Even today harvest festivals exercise an attraction even in the most urban of parishes surrounded by brick for miles and without a field or a farm within its boundaries. Where is the corresponding affirmation of God at work within the industrial process? A piece of coal amidst the apples in the sanctuary, or a cog wheel among the chrysanthemums is nothing more than a reluctant admission that our lives today depend upon coal and cogs, upon oil and computers as much as upon crops and cattle. We need a joyful celebration of the worth of the industrial undertaking, a celebration which must have its religious aspect. When a festival of industry touches our hearts as deeply as does harvest festival, then we shall have overcome our sickness.

—The Bishop of Ripon (England), "Faith in Business,"
Work in Worship

WORKPLACE PRAYER

Ever-present God, I give you thanks for the world of work of which I am a part. Along with sustaining the land by water and wind, you supply the means by which we live in an industrial and service society. I thank you for the people who provide for the needs of this workplace—the office supplies, tools, raw products, consulting, and professional services that enable work to run smoothly. I thank you for the people with whom I work—all of us who are working together to meet the needs of our business, our customers, and ourselves. Bless the hard work that goes into making this place function. And bless me in the job I do today. Amen.

—WDT

Transforming the Earth

Businesses should have a specific goal: to provide goods and services which actually contribute to the cultural enrichment of the earth and human society, or to provide goods and services which aid others toward this goal. It is not enough that a business merely makes a profit (though culturally faithful businesses may turn a profit). And it is not the purpose of businesses to be productive as an end in itself (though businesses should certainly be productive). Businesses fit in best with God's cultural program when they are oriented toward the ultimate goal to transform the earth into a glorious city full of goodness, beauty and truth. In order to achieve this lofty goal, we must grow in our understanding of God's standards for the good, the true, and the beautiful, so we can incorporate these values in our products, no matter how trivial or mundane. The business world is in desperate need of this big picture.

—David Bruce Hegeman, "The Business of Making Culture,"
Business Reform

Unless the Lord builds the house, those who build it labor in vain.

—*Psalm 127:1*

WORKPLACE PRAYER

Whether we work at home or at school, in a factory or an office,
   indoors or out of doors, we give our work to you, Lord God.
Whether we work alone or with others, with hand or brain,
   in a shop or in a hospital, we give our work to you, Lord God.
Whether our work is paid or unpaid, interesting or boring,
   with computers or with people, we give our work to you, Lord God.
Whether our work involves manufacturing or planning,
   travelling or home making, teaching, learning or caring,
   we give our work to you, Lord God.
Whatever we do, give us a sense of wonder.
Whatever we make, give us a sense of achievement.
Whatever we build, grant us a sense of glory.
Whatever our work, grant us a share in your purpose.
   In the name of Jesus Christ we pray. Amen.

—*Faith in Business*

A Job Well Done

If a man is called to be a street sweeper, he should sweep streets even as Michaelangelo painted, or Beethoven composed music, or Shakespeare wrote poetry. He should sweep streets so well that all the hosts of heaven and earth will pause to say, here lived a great street sweeper who did his job well.

—Martin Luther King, Jr.

WORKPLACE PRAYER

O God, I am moved by these words of one who challenged a whole race of people—a whole nation—to excellence. I want to embody excellence in my work. I also know that the category of my job or the amount of my income does not matter to you; only that I work in such a way that you and the hosts of heaven rejoice at how I do my work. As I do the tasks before me today, I call on your help. I thank you that you have given me the skills to do my job, and I pray that you will help me use them for your honor. Amen.

—WDT

Finally, beloved, whatever is true, whatever is honorable, whatever is just, whatever is pure, whatever is pleasing, whatever is commendable, if there is any excellence and if there is anything worthy of praise, think about these things. Keep on doing the things that you have learned and received and heard and seen in me, and the God of peace will be with you.

—Philippians 4:8-9

Living in God's Spirit

Spirit to me is the indefinable thing that makes human life so wonderful. It's the sense of love, of anticipation; it's the beauty of life. It's the thing that gives you an extra-special joy, like the singular joy you get when you see your children succeeding and doing well. Spirit is getting up in the morning and seeing that it's a beautiful day and thanking God that you're alive and that you have the ability to participate. I think spirit is also a sense of hope and optimism that, no matter how bad things are, they may get better. I think that's very much a part of the human spirit. I think that's what human beings contribute to the world.

—Rudolph Giuliani, in *What Is Spirit?*

WORKPLACE PRAYER

O God of Beauty, I thank you that you have created so many amazing things in this world. Help me to feel alive in it today. Help me to contribute strength and beauty to your creation. Help me especially to be aware of the connections I share with each person I encounter. And if I run into anger or conflict or difficult tasks, remind me that nothing is able to separate me from your love. Bless me with a sense of joy in all that I do, for the sake of Jesus Christ, in whose name I offer this prayer, and myself. Amen.

—WDT

On-the-Job Prayer

27

The spirit of God has made me, and the breath of the Almighty gives me life.

—Job 33:4

*Now we have received
not the spirit of
the world, but the
Spirit that is from
God, so that we may
understand the gifts
bestowed on us by
God.*

—1 Corinthians 2:12

Let Your Light Shine

Since I was a very young girl, the Holy Spirit has been a real guiding light in my life. For me, it's so easy to understand, but it can be difficult to explain it to someone else. In my experience, when you are filled with spirit it is contagious. It's like an eternal flame that people are drawn to. It's the smile from you that someone needs and didn't expect, generous giving without expecting something in return, when you're singing a song or communicating with an audience, the ability to get out of the way and let the Spirit move through you to someone else. To me, spirit is that light that shines so bright in people's eyes. One of the greatest things about spirit is that it doesn't notice the color of a person's skin, what religion they belong to, their age, or their financial status. I couldn't imagine life without the Holy Spirit, for spirit is life and life is spirit.

—Florence Henderson, in *What Is Spirit?*

WORKPLACE PRAYER

Giver of Gifts, thank you for the work you have given me to do today. May your Spirit in me be contagious in my workplace. Keep me from confining your gifts. Help me to become more aware of the ways your light shines in my workplace: in the smiles of people I meet, in the concern for excellence I see around me, and in the help I receive from others. Thank you that your Spirit is always there to guide me. Amen.

—WDT

Spiritual Values

There is a "change of mind" taking place in the modern world that is reflected in demographic survey data, in the new values emphasis of the women's movement, in the ecological, peace, and alternative lifestyles movements, in the Green political movements in various countries, and in the suddenly rising interest in various "twelve-step" programs for dealing with addictions and co-dependency. This change of mind is characterized by a repudiation of the competitive, exploitive materialism and consumerism of modern society, with an increased emphasis on alternative values. These values include improved quality of relationships, cooperation, caring and nurturing, oneness of humanity, social justice, humane ecological and spiritual values, as well as respect and caring for the other creatures on the planet.

—Willis Harman, "Twenty-First Century Business,"
New Traditions in Business

WORKPLACE PRAYER

Thank you, God, that there is a wind of change abroad, away from materialism toward spiritual values. Show me how I can reflect your values today. I want to care for those less fortunate, but I find myself focusing on getting the tasks on my "to do" list accomplished. I want to honor the earth and be a steward of its resources, but it is all too easy to focus on how quickly I can get somewhere. I want to love and respect those in my family, but I'm quick to get angry at the little things they do that rub me the wrong way. I want to keep my body healthy, but I find myself too tired or too busy to do anything about it. Continue to teach me your way to live. Show me how to act with integrity and generosity, to work conscientiously. Remind me today that, as I give to others, I give to you. Amen.

—WDT

On-the-Job Prayer

29

If your enemies are hungry, feed them; if they are thirsty, give them something to drink; for by doing this you will heap burning coals on their heads. Do not be overcome by evil, but overcome evil with good.

—Romans 12:20-21

*Where two or three
are gathered in my
name, I am there
among them.*

—Matthew 18:20

Between Sundays

Christianity is made for the road, not the sanctuary! Christianity took root where the only sanctuary was a Jewish temple or synagogue, and very soon the church was driven from both. For three centuries Christian faith was propagated in homes and marketplaces, prisons and catacombs. Even with the coming of the great cathedrals and throughout the medieval period, fellowship continued in the home and the marketplace. Worship happened whenever Christians were able to meet, under whatever circumstance, wherever they were.

The sanctuary is a fact of contemporary Christianity which is probably here to stay, but the caricature of worship is the idea that it is limited to a special place at a particular time in a peculiar way, and usually dependent upon a "professional" for leadership. Lost is the spontaneity of primitive Christian worship, and with it, more often than not, the power and relevance of faith to life. Authentic Christianity is designed for the home and the community, the office and the shop, the club and the campus, the market, factory and farm. Christianity is for every day, wherever one is, under whatever circumstances. Christianity is for between Sundays!

—Richard C. Halverson, former U.S. Senate Chaplain,
Walk with God between Sundays

WORKPLACE PRAYER

Almighty God, whose Son Jesus Christ in his earthly life shared our toil and hallowed our labor: Be present with your people where they work; make those who carry on the industries and commerce of this land responsive to your will; and give to us all a pride in what we do, and a just return for our labor; through Jesus Christ our Lord, who lives and reigns with you, in the unity of the Holy Spirit, one God, now and for ever. Amen.

—*Book of Common Prayer*

What Are You Doing?

What in God's name are you doing? Until you've intentionally thought of your life as a call, there are some potential problems with this pithily put question. One is that we too often equate Christian call with the specific vocation of ordained ministry—a vital and noble profession, but not for everyone.... As a teacher told me as I prepared for ordination, "Your vocation is the last stand for the dedicated generalist."

If you're drawn to the life of faith in the community of faith, you should in God's name develop a whole, rounded, practicing vocation. A Christian being should be able to greet a seeker, quote the gospel, listen to pain, feed the hungry, sing a simple hymn, give to and build up the local church (and know why), find a daily minute to be quiet and know Whose you are, think about what the church means for others and not for you alone, speak truth to power, act with others, practice hospitality, be able to love God and your neighbor at the same time, "out" yourself as a believer without being obnoxious, comfort the dying, house the homeless, just for starters. In God's name, whole living is not for the faint of heart.

—William McD. Tully, St. Bartholomew's Church, New York

The fruit of the Spirit is love, joy, peace, patience, kindness, generosity, faithfulness, gentleness, and self-control.

—*Galatians 5:22*

WORKPLACE PRAYER

Heavenly Father, in you we live and move and have our being. We humbly pray that you so guide and govern us by your Holy Spirit that in all the cares and occupations of our life we may not forget you but may remember that we are ever walking in your sight; through Jesus Christ our Lord. Amen.

—*Book of Common Prayer*

Looking to Jesus the pioneer and perfecter of our faith, who for the sake of the joy that was set before him endured the cross, disregarding its shame, and has taken his seat at the right hand of the throne of God.

—Hebrews 12:2

God's Call

Vocation comes from the Latin *vocare*, "to call," and means the work a person is called to by God. There are all different kinds of voices calling you to all different kinds of work, and the problem is to find out which is the voice of God rather than of society, say, or the superego, or self-interest.

By and large a good rule for finding out is this: The kind of work God usually calls you to is the kind of work (a) that you need to do and (b) that the world needs to have done. If you really get a kick out of your work, you've presumably met requirement (a), but if your work is writing cigarette ads, the chances are you've missed requirement (b). On the other hand, if your work is being a doctor in a leper colony, you have probably met requirement (b), but if most of the time you're bored and depressed by it, the chances are you have not only surpassed (a), but probably aren't helping your patients much either.

Neither the hair shirt nor the soft berth will do. The place God calls you to is the place where your deep gladness and the world's deep hunger meet.

—Frederick Buechner, *Beyond Words*

WORKPLACE PRAYER

Counselor and Friend, I ask for a spirit of reflectiveness. Help me today to see my work through the lens of what the world needs. Where my work is able to meet the deep hunger of society, I thank you. Where I am missing the mark, increase my awareness and shift my focus. Help me to truly see where my work gives me gladness—and where it is generating frustration, depression or avoidance. Where there is a mismatch, guide me, I pray, to your will in dealing with it. I ask this in the name of Jesus who knew what God had called him to do and did it "for the sake of the joy that was set before him." Amen.

—WDT

At the Center of God's Mission

I want to challenge a theology and a history which automatically assumes…that what we do as Christians in the church is more significant in our discipleship than what we do in our daily activity as executives, university professors, engineers, lawyers and so on. We need to see at the center of God's mission not the splendid work of church life, but the equally splendid wilderness of the world—where there are few places for Christians to hide, where moral and ethical signposts are blurred or nonexistent, and where we are outnumbered by the indifferent, the unholy, and the cultured despisers of our day.

I am proposing…a start from a wholly new perspective. That is: not to seek survival as an institution but to aim to be the church of Jesus Christ in the world. So the TV producer will consider how, exactly, she or he brings Christianity into the presentation of programs; the engineer will reflect on his or her design, professional relationships, and influence on others from a Christian standpoint; the corporate director will view the policy proposals of management within a perspective of servant-leadership.

—George Carey, former Archbishop of Canterbury,
"Empowering the Priesthood of All Believers"

And he said to them, "Go into all the world and proclaim the good news to the whole creation."

—Mark 16:15

WORKPLACE PRAYER

Hope of the World, it is easy to feel that my faith gets lost in the wilderness of confused values in today's world. Help me to see that this "splendid wilderness" is the center of your mission. Show me today how I can be an extension of your hand in this world, a reflection of your love for all people. Help me to use whatever role I play in the workplace to move the world toward justice, righteousness and peace. Use me in whatever way you can to achieve your creative and redemptive purposes for humankind. Show me how to do my part. Amen.

—WDT

Thus he has shown the mercy promised to our ancestors, and has remembered his holy covenant, the oath that he swore to our ancestor Abraham, to grant us that we, being rescued from the hands of our enemies, might serve him without fear, in holiness and righteousness before him all our days.

—Luke 1:72-75

A Place of Holiness

Work is not to be merely tolerated; it is a call to complete the work of creation and to cooperate in the work of redemption. Work itself must become a way to God, not merely an interlude between morning and evening prayers. In fact, prayer cannot be defined as time snatched from the messy world…. Every bed made, potato peeled, or ton of steel poured is the incense of praise rising about the suburban chimney and the black clouds of the steel mill. For a full-time Christian, a spirituality that is practiced in a state of activity is preferable to, if not superior to, any spirituality that is practiced in a state of withdrawal. An incense-filled chapel is not more holy than a smoke-filled caucus room…. A sin-scarred world is, for the full-time Christian, as much a place for holiness as any sanctuary.

—William Droel, *Full-Time Christians*

WORKPLACE PRAYER

O God, it is hard for me to think of my workplace as holy. There is so much about my job that seems removed from the highest and best of heaven and earth. The thought that my work has anything to do with your work of creation does not come easily. Yet your hand in the world is a creative hand, providing ever new forms of usefulness and beauty. I don't often think of my work as redemptive, either, but I trust that you can use what my co-workers and I do to change the world for the better. So, God, thank you for calling me to this job as a vocation to carry on your divine plan for this world. Help me to serve you today in holiness. Amen.

—WDT

Perseverance

If I had to select one quality, one personal characteristic that I regard as being most highly correlated with success, whatever the field, I would pick the trait of persistence. Determination. The will to endure to the end, to get knocked down seventy times and get up off the floor saying, here comes number seventy-one!

—Richard M. DeVos, co-founder of Amway Corporation

WORKPLACE PRAYER

Persistent God, you know that sometimes I just don't feel up to the task. Sometimes I feel as if I've been plodding along for too long, getting bogged down instead of getting results. Today I need your strength, your vision, your persistence to do the work that needs to be done. Help me not to glory in the finish, but to honor you in the continuing. Remind me that you are in the journey as much as in the finish. I trust in your faithfulness and call on your inspiration to make a difference in my work this day. Amen.

—WDT

Therefore, since we are surrounded by so great a cloud of witnesses, let us also lay aside every weight and the sin that clings so closely, and let us run with perseverance the race that is set before us.

—*Hebrews 12:1*

*Let me hear of your
steadfast love in the
morning, for in you I
put my trust. Teach
me the way I should
go, for to you I lift up
my soul.*

—*Psalm 143:8*

Antidote to Lethargy

When you combine the spiritual and the intellectual in your work, you develop a natural flexibility that enables you to move quickly and respond to unexpected situations. There will be times when you become mired in the practical unfolding of your work. When this happens, the view becomes one-dimensional and you lose the malleability of movement that allows you to adjust appropriately to challenging circumstances. Without this resilience, spontaneity disappears because the tendency is to stay put and not move. Some of the antidotes to lethargy are prayer, play, walking, exercise of any kind, enjoying the company of children, and being with friends and those who love you. Recognize that it's a temporary phase and will pass.

—Michael and Justine Willis Toms, *True Work*

WORKPLACE PRAYER

Dear God, you know how tightly I sometimes hold on to the tasks at hand. Sometimes I worry about the details too much, and I try to control everything. Sometimes I don't trust my co-workers to do their part, and I try to do too much myself. Release me, I pray, from having to be in control. Open me to your insight about my work. Use my resources and skills for the best possible outcome. Help me to honor my co-workers and their abilities, and give me the flexibility to change. I place all my tasks in your hands. When my view gets one-sided, teach me resilience. When I get bogged down, help me rediscover spontaneity. When I am filled with tension, help me remember to take time for play, to enjoy my family and friends. Above all, open my heart to your love. Amen.

—WDT

For the Glory of God

I have already, on a previous occasion, spoken at some length on the subject of work and vocation. What I urged then was a thoroughgoing revolution in our whole attitude to work. I asked that it should be looked upon—not as a necessary drudgery to be undergone for the purpose of making money, but as a way of life in which the nature of man should find its proper exercise and delight and so fulfill itself to the glory of God. That it should, in fact, be thought of as a creative activity undertaken for the love of the work itself; and that man, made in God's image, should make things, as God makes them. for the sake of doing well a thing that is well worth doing.

—Dorothy Sayers, *Why Work?*

*Whatever you do,
do everything for the
glory of God.*

—1 Corinthians
10:31

WORKPLACE PRAYER

Creator of heaven and earth, the idea that my work is an extension of your work is a wonderful thought. I confess that sometimes my work feels like drudgery—parts of it anyway—however interesting it may be at times and however much money it produces. Help me today when I get bogged down to remember that you made the world, you made me in your image, and you brought me to this job. I ask you to give me the energy and insight to do it well. I pray that my work today will be to your glory. Amen.

—WDT

On-the-Job Prayer

38

Do not boast about tomorrow, for you do not know what a day may bring.

—*Proverbs 27:1*

The Price of a Day

This is a new day. God has given me this day to use as I will. I can waste it or use it for good, but what I do today is important because I am exchanging a day of my life for it! When tomorrow comes, this day will be gone forever, leaving in its place something that I have traded for it. I want it to be gain and not loss; good and not evil; success and not failure, in order that I shall not regret the price I have paid for it.

—Author unknown

WORKPLACE PRAYER

O God, receive my thanks for the great gift of today. Renew me by your Spirit for whatever the day will bring. I pray not only for myself but for all who will perform valuable services today and all who will make important products. I pray for homemakers who perform tasks vital to the family, for professional persons who bring long and expensive preparation to the service they render to others, for workers in thankless tasks without whom our world would not work, for persons who serve in government, education, manufacturing, health care, law enforcement and varieties of jobs people know little about. Give all who serve society genuine love, strength, wisdom, and the sense that all their work is an integral part of your work and purpose for the world. I offer myself as a worker to you, with the prayer that this day may be a good one in every way. Receive this prayer, Lord, in the name of Jesus, the living Christ, who is my companion in this workplace today and every day. Amen.

—Author unknown

The Eyes of God

If we are alert to seeking the face of God, to discerning his presence in the faces of our colleagues, clients, companions and competitors, the reality of God's presence in the marketplace will strike us more frequently. Take the eyes. Jesus explained that "your eye is the lamp of the body; if your eye is healthy, your whole body is full of light; but if it is not healthy, your body is full of darkness. Therefore consider whether the light in you is not darkness."

It is a small step to switch our thinking about our own eyes—and the eyes of those around us—to the eyes of God. As we watch others and others watch us, so God watches everyone. "For the eyes of the Lord range throughout the entire earth, to strengthen those whose heart is true to him." This watchfulness is underlined again: "Truly the eye of the Lord is on those who fear him, on those who hope in his steadfast love, to deliver their soul from death and to keep them alive in famine." That is a promise on which to focus when workplace realities threaten our spiritual survival and our material well-being.

—David Prior, "Practicing God's Presence at Work," *Faith at Work*

I will instruct you and teach you the way you should go; I will counsel you with my eye upon you.

—Psalm 32:8

WORKPLACE PRAYER

Give to me, O God, a clear and watchful eye.
Give to me, O God, a firm but gentle touch.
Give to me, O God, a good receptive ear.
Give to me, O God, a clean discerning taste.
Give to me, O God, a subtle sense of smell.
Give to me, O God, an openness to others.
Give to me, O God, an awareness now of you.
Give to me, O God, each thing that is needful for my body.
Give to me, O God, that which will renew my mind.
Give to me, O God, that which will strengthen my spirit.
Give to me, O God, healing for my sickness.
Give to me, O God, repentance for my sins.
Give to me, O God, yourself above all else.

—Author unknown

~~~~~~

*Therefore I tell you,
do not worry about
your life, what you
will eat, or what you
will drink, or about
your body, what you
will wear. Is not life
more than food and
the body more than
clothing?*

—*Matthew 6:25*

Handling Stress

Life is stressful. Unless you've managed to get away from it all, retiring to some idyllic island, you're surely experiencing stress on a regular basis. And even on that island you might begin to worry about something—say, coconuts falling on your head. There's always something. In a way, you need stress. When you finally get rid of all the stress in your life, you'll be dead. Our daily challenges keep us going. Some people say they thrive on stress. Without a deadline to meet, some nearly impossible task to perform, or a major life drama unfolding—they get bored. When things are too quiet, they worry about what's not happening and why. Some people even stir things up at home or at work as part of an unconscious need for excitement. In the last generation, the world has learned a great deal about the negative effects of stress. High stress can do a number on your heart, raising your blood pressure. It can put a damper on your immune system, making you susceptible to all sorts of diseases. Can you accept it and move on, or do you make things worse by worrying or diving into some self-destructive habit?

—Thomas Whiteman and Randy Petersen, *Stress Test*

~~~~~~

WORKPLACE PRAYER

Compassionate God, you know how I react to stress. I may not experience it all the time, and I may not always show it, but stress is real in this workplace. I think of the words of the psalmist, "Be still and know that I am God." That's harder than it sounds, God, especially the "be still" part. So I am asking you to give me whatever it takes to stay calm and take the day as it comes. I know that you are God, and I trust that you will never fail me. Now help me make this truth define who I am and how I deal with whatever stress may come along. I trust that your everlasting arms are underneath me, and with your help I will get through it all. Amen.

—WDT

Striking a Balance

How much better to get wisdom than gold!
    To get understanding is to be chosen rather than silver.
The highway of the upright avoids evil;
    those who guard their way preserve their lives.
Pride goes before destruction
    and a haughty spirit before a fall.
It is better to be of a lowly spirit among the poor
    than to divide the spoil with the proud.
Those who are attentive to a matter will prosper,
    and happy are those who trust in the Lord.

—Proverbs 16:16-20

WORKPLACE PRAYER

God of Wisdom, you alone know my deepest thoughts. You know that I need money to live, but you also know the thoughts and desires that drive my quest for money. Help me to balance my quest for gold with my need for your wisdom. Help me today, in every decision, in every encounter, in every action, to be attentive to your wisdom and to trust in you. Keep me humble in spirit and enable me to be who you want me to be. Thank you for the ways in which you bring prosperity into my life—both in your care for my physical needs and your sustaining support for my spiritual and emotional needs. Amen.

—WDT

On-the-Job Prayer

41

Trust in the Lord, and do good; so you will live in the land, and enjoy security. Take delight in the Lord, and he will give you the desires of your heart. Commit your way to the Lord; trust in him, and he will act.

—Psalm 37:3-5

What gain have the
workers from
their toil?

I have seen the
business that
God has given
to everyone to be
busy with.

He has made
everything
suitable for its
time;

moreover he has put a
sense of past and
future into their
minds.

—Ecclesiastes 3:
9-11a

God's Timing

For everything there is a season, and a time for every matter under heaven:
a time to be born, and a time to die;
a time to plant, and a time to pluck up what is planted;
a time to kill, and a time to heal;
a time to break down, and a time to build up;
a time to weep, and a time to laugh;
a time to mourn, and a time to dance;
a time to throw away stones, and a time to gather stones together;
a time to embrace, and a time to refrain from embracing,
a time to seek, and a time to lose;
a time to keep, and a time to throw away;
a time to tear, and a time to sew;
a time to keep silence, and a time to speak;
a time to love, and a time to hate;
a time for war, and a time for peace.

—Ecclesiastes 3:1-8

WORKPLACE PRAYER

Steadfast God, you know that I sometimes lose track of time. The clock is clear enough, but what I can do with this time or that is not always evident. I sometimes get it wrong, and I end up spending too much time on what doesn't matter—or too little time on what's important. Forgive me. Help me to be especially aware today that you are the source and purpose of my work, that you are involved in the details of my work, that it is not just a way to make a living. Thank you also for the assurance that you have "a sense of past and future." Keep me in touch with your sense of things; I need your perspective to sort out the times and seasons of life. Amen.

—WDT

Work with Purpose

By his life Jesus Christ redeemed our daily life and by his work made all our work blessed. His birth was witnessed by shepherds who took time off work to attend his birth. He worked as a carpenter. He invited ordinary fishermen to become extraordinary fishers for and with God. He told stories of farm workers and homemakers, invited tax collectors to become disciples, and saw worth in work that others despised. He cooked the disciples' Easter breakfast. By his work he taught us to see God's glory in ordinary events. By his ministry he showed us that compassion is our life work. By his vocation he followed God's will and invited us to follow him. By his death and resurrection he redeemed us and revealed that our work is never lost, never without purpose, never worthless. So in remembrance of the mighty acts of Jesus Christ, we offer ourselves as workers in his mission and promise in our workplace and our daily life to witness the truth that Jesus Christ is Lord.

—Worship & Daily Life

WORKPLACE PRAYER

Direct us, O Lord, in all our doings with your most gracious favor, and further us with your continual help; that in all our works begun, continued, and ended in you, we may glorify your holy name, and finally, by your mercy, obtain everlasting life; through Jesus Christ our Lord. Amen.

—Book of Common Prayer

On-the-Job Prayer

43

For us there is one God, the Father, from whom are all things and for whom we exist, and one Lord, Jesus Christ, through whom are all things and through whom we exist.

—1 Corinthians 8:6

Awake, awake, put on strength…so the ransomed of the Lord shall return, and come to Zion with singing; everlasting joy shall be upon their heads; they shall obtain joy and gladness, and sorrow and sighing shall flee away.

—Isaiah 51:9-11

Monday Morning

"Every Monday morning I follow the same pattern. My alarm goes off and I push the snooze button once, and then a second time. It's Monday and the last thing I want to do is get up and go to work. While I'm in the shower, I am actually hoping the traffic is so heavy that my arrival at work will be delayed."

Many people can identify with that sad lament from a mid-level manager in the Los Angeles area. For them, the term work denotes a burden, a drudgery, a grindstone, something they have to toil away at and which limits their quality personal time. Yet for others, work is an activity that is energizing, motivating and fulfilling. For them, it is the road to appreciation, achievement, identity and income. Some even view their work as a mission or life-calling. The fact is that most of us need and want to work. Since we spend so much time working, it's to our advantage to enjoy what we do.

—Victor M. Parachin, *Positive Thinking Magazine*

WORKPLACE PRAYER

O God of New Beginnings, I thank you for each Monday morning. You give me strength to get up and get going, even though it is sometimes a struggle. You give me the resources to live my life and to do my work: a mind to think and to make decisions, eyes to see and ears to hear, a body that I can move from place to place. And you have given me the capacity to enjoy what I do. Keep me grateful this day for my job and for your loving presence, whatever the day may bring. Amen.

—WDT

The Pursuit of Happiness

America has been called the only nation founded on a good idea. That idea has been given many and elaborate explanations, but the most concise and familiar formulation is the pursuit of happiness. For a fortunate few people, happiness is the pursuit of excellence in a vocation. The vocation can be a profession or a craft, elite or common, poetry or carpentry. What matters most is an idea of excellence against which to measure achievement. Fortunate people have a talent for happiness. Possession of any talent can help a person toward happiness. As Aristotle said, happiness is not a condition that is produced or stands on its own; rather, it is a frame of mind that accompanies an activity. But another frame of mind comes first. It is a steely determination to do well.

—George F. Will, *Men at Work*

WORKPLACE PRAYER

Holy One, I know you want the best for me, you want me to be happy. But I confess that what I do—at least some of the time—doesn't always bring happiness to me or to those around me. By your Spirit, help me to see beyond the work itself to the quality of what I do. Give me a clear vision today that my work calls for excellence, whether I'm doing something that will affect the success of the business, or performing a task that some might see as small and insignificant. Bless me with the true happiness that comes from having done my best to honor you. Amen.

—WDT

Happy is everyone who fears the Lord, who walks in his ways. You shall eat the fruit of the labor of your hands; you shall be happy, and it shall go well with you.

—Psalm 128:1-2

Character produces hope, and hope does not disappoint us, because God's love has been poured into our hearts through the Holy Spirit that has been given to us.

—Romans 5:4b-5

Laboring with Character

Be practical as well as generous in your ideals; keep your eyes on the stars and keep your feet on the ground. Courage, hard work, self-mastery and intelligent effort are all essential to a successful life. Character in the long run is the decisive factor in the life of an individual and of nations alike.

—Theodore Roosevelt

WORKPLACE PRAYER

O God of Excellence, I am grateful that you love me and accept me just as I am. But I also am acutely aware of how often I fall short. Thank you that you hold me to a higher standard. Walk with me today as I try to live the life of Christ in my work. Help me to practice generosity, courage, and intelligent effort—to be a person of character. And, especially, help me to embody your spirit of love, even toward those who rub me the wrong way or criticize me or challenge me. I praise you with the psalmist that your "steadfast love is higher than the heavens." Amen.

—WDT

Dealing with Difficult People

All work, whether it is ideal or not, will require you to put your spiritual and psychological skills into practice. When work involves interactions with others, then we will be challenged to live the most basic of principles we have learned, such as kindness, patience, prudence, truthfulness, perseverance and humility. Even if your work situation is the best of the best, all these principles must be brought to bear in everyday contacts. Often it is through sharing painful situations with others that we attain deeper levels of emotional and spiritual maturity. You may notice how your life has blossomed with greater confidence because you've dealt successfully with difficulties.

—Michael and Justine Willis Toms, *True Work*

You shall love the Lord your God with all your heart, and with all your soul, and with all your strength, and with all your mind; and your neighbor as yourself.

—Luke 10:27

WORKPLACE PRAYER

Loving God, I hope that I don't have to deal with any difficult people today, but that may be too much to expect. Help me realize how much some people are hurting. Help me see past their hurtful behaviors to their hurting souls. Give me an understanding heart, a big dose of patience, and the ability to let go of any desire to retaliate. Give me your love for those around me—even the hard-to-work with. I am grateful that love can turn around even the most painful situation or difficult conflict. Walk with me today. Amen.

—WDT

People go out to their work and to their labor until the evening. O Lord, how manifold are your works! In wisdom you have made them all.

—*Psalm 104:23-24*

Putting Wisdom to Work

A soft answer turns away wrath,
　　but a harsh word stirs up anger.
The tongue of the wise dispenses knowledge,
　　but the mouths of fools pour out folly.
The eyes of the Lord are in every place,
　　keeping watch on the evil and the good.
A gentle tongue is a tree of life,
　　but perverseness in it breaks the spirit.

—Proverbs 15:1-4

WORKPLACE PRAYER

Holy One, this ancient wisdom about a soft answer and a gentle tongue seems to be just for me and for my workplace. As I ponder it, show me by your Spirit the ways I have been guilty of arrogance and carelessness of tongue, of being a lesser person than you want me to be. Show me how to embody this wisdom in my work today. When I feel critical of my co-workers, help me to understand their circumstances. When I feel angry about a problem, turn my mind to solutions. When I get irritated with someone, gentle my tongue and my attitude. I want to know and to do your will in all my relationships on this job, and I need your help. Thank you for being in every place, in every conversation, in every action of this day. Amen.

—WDT

Whatever You Do

Bear with one another and, if anyone has a complaint against another, forgive each other; just as the Lord has forgiven you, so you also must forgive. Above all, clothe yourselves with love, which binds everything together in perfect harmony. And let the peace of Christ rule in your hearts, to which indeed you were called in the one body. And be thankful. Let the word of Christ dwell in you richly; teach and admonish one another in all wisdom; and with gratitude in your hearts sing psalms, hymns, and spiritual songs to God. And whatever you do, in word or deed, do everything in the name of the Lord Jesus, giving thanks to God the Father through him.

—Colossians 3:13-17

WORKPLACE PRAYER

Let me not wander in vain.
Let me not labor in vain.
Let me not mingle with the prejudiced.
Let me not leave the company of the virtuous.
Let me not fly into anger.
Let me not stray off the path of goodness.
Let me not seek for this day or for the morrow.
Give me such a wealth, O Almighty!

—Pattinattar (tenth-century poet)

So let us not grow weary in doing what is right, for we will reap at harvest time, if we do not give up. So then, whenever we have an opportunity, let us work for the good of all, and especially for those of the family of faith.

—Galatians 6:9-10

*If you forgive others
their trespasses, your
heavenly Father will
also forgive you; but
if you do not forgive
others, neither will
your Father forgive
your trespasses.*

—Matthew 6:14-15

"I'm Sorry"

Apology and forgiveness go together. Typically one follows the other. I apologize to you, and you forgive me. Apology and forgiveness have become something of a neglected art in today's fast-paced world. In the workplace, especially, petty irritations and hurts often cry out for resolution. Especially in larger companies, intrigue, deception, and malicious gossip are all too common. My good friend, Sylvia Boorstein, shared with me "the nine words that would change the world," which she learned from Rabbi David Zeller. The nine words are "I'm sorry. I made a mistake. Please forgive me." If we all made it a point to practice some form of these nine words, so that they dwelled in our heart, I have no doubt that it would indeed begin to change the world. There is an intimacy and magnetism to apology and forgiveness that breaks down the barriers between people and draws them closer. That intimacy is difficult to regain in the modern workplace, where strangers are often thrust together in impersonal cubicles. But through our spiritual intention and sustained effort, each of us can bring that spirit back to life.

—Lewis Richmond, *Work as a Spiritual Practice*

⟶≡≡≡≡⟶

WORKPLACE PRAYER

Merciful God, you know there are times when I find it difficult or impossible to forgive. Sometimes my pride gets in the way, and it is hard for me. Sometimes I hold onto my anger. Help me today, by your Spirit, to convey your gift of forgiveness. Remind me that the whole process of forgiving begins not with me but with you. For you offer the world and every person I will meet today your forgiveness through Jesus Christ our Lord. Amen.

—WDT

Being Gracious on the Job

You may be the most talented person in your company at your job description, but if you aren't gracious, too, you may just seem like noise to the people around you. Who can stand someone who toots his own horn (or clangs her own cymbal) so much that others can't wait to get away from the sound?

Obnoxiousness isn't part of a Christian's job description. The hallmarks of faith are graciousness and love. So when you do well in your work, thank God for the gifts he's given you that allow you to serve him well. Be thankful that he's given folks who helped you learn your job and who continue to make your work possible. And appreciate the particular gifts of others who work with you.

No matter how gifted you are spiritually or skill-wise, no one appreciates someone who's so full of himself that there's no room for God or anyone else. So have some love on your job, and you won't just be noise; you'll shed the light of Jesus' love.

—Pamela McQuade, *Daily Wisdom for the Workplace*

*Do to others as you
would have them do
to you.*

—Luke 6:27

WORKPLACE PRAYER

Dearest Lord, teach me to be generous;
Teach me to serve thee as thou deservest;
To give and not to count the cost,
To fight and not to heed the wounds,
To toil and not to seek for rest,
To labor and not to ask for any reward,
Save that of knowing that I do thy will.
Amen.

—St. Ignatius of Loyola (1491-1556)

*Glory in his holy
name; let the hearts
of those who seek the
Lord rejoice. Seek
the Lord and his
strength, seek his
presence continually.*

*—1 Chronicles
16:10-11*

Attitude Adjustment

Brother Lawrence, author of the little Christian classic, *The Practice
of the Presence of God*, spent a substantial part of his working life as a
lay brother in the kitchen of a Carmelite monastery in Burgundy. He
did not enjoy the work and he was "a great awkward fellow who broke
everything." But he gradually developed an attitude to his daily life, in
which the presence of God became as real in work as in prayer. His
advice is: "We must, during all our labor and in all else that we do...
pause for some short moment, as often indeed as we can, to worship
God in the depth of our heart, to savor him, though it be but in passing,
and as it were by stealth. To savor him...by stealth presents each of us
with a challenge and an incentive."

—The Centre for Marketplace Theology

WORKPLACE PRAYER

**Breathe in me, O Holy Spirit,
That my thoughts may all be holy.
Act in me, O Holy Spirit,
That my work may be holy.
Draw my heart, O Holy Spirit,
That I love but what is holy.
Strengthen me, O Holy Spirit,
To defend all that is holy.
Guard me, O Holy Spirit,
That I always may be holy.**

—St. Augustine (354-430)

When Life is Unfair

"It's not fair!" We've all wanted to cry that at some point in our careers. No matter how dedicated we are to our work, at some point we'll face a situation where we feel we've been treated unfairly, whether we have to give up a vacation week we really wanted or don't get the job transfer we applied for. When that happens, how do we react? Do we take it out on the company in subtle ways, not working as hard as we used to or taking home a few "extra" pencils for the kids?

It's a natural response to feel hurt when we don't get something we wanted badly. Our hopes are dashed when something enjoyable falls through. But that doesn't mean we have the right to retaliate. Returning evil for evil just puts more evil in the world. But being aboveboard and honest, even when things don't go our way, will return good to the world.

Maybe it's not fair. Maybe you deserved that vacation or transfer. But obeying God will bring good out of unfairness. All you have to do is give your employer the fairness you never got.

Do not repay anyone evil for evil, but take thought for what is noble in the sight of all.

—Romans 12:17

—Pamela McQuade, *Daily Wisdom for the Workplace*

WORKPLACE PRAYER

Lord, I know what unfairness is like,
And I hate to be on its receiving end.
But when life is unfair,
Help me to turn it to good
As a testimony to right.
Amen.

—Pamela McQuade, *Daily Wisdom for the Workplace*

On-the-Job Prayer

54

Be strong and of good courage, and act. Do not be afraid or dismayed; for the Lord God, my God, is with you. He will not fail you or forsake you, until all the work for the service of the house of the Lord is finished.

—1 Chronicles 28:20

Reshaping Stress

Work without meaning is deadly. In the United States, stress-related diseases such as ulcers, high blood pressure and heart attacks cost the U.S. economy 200 billion dollars per year in absenteeism, compensation claims, and medical expenses. A recent report by the United Nations International Labor Organization labels job stress "one of the most serious health issues of the twentieth century." Calling job stress "a global phenomenon," the report found that blue collar and women workers especially suffer from job stress. It recommends that individual workers deal with stress through relaxation techniques such as yoga, exercise, diet, counseling, and change of attitude; at the same time employers are urged to give employees more control over their work worlds. People need a spiritual sense of work.

—Matthew Fox, *The Reinvention of Work*

WORKPLACE PRAYER

Holy Comforter, I am grateful for those in the work world who are becoming more sensitive to the emotional and spiritual needs of workers. I thank you for the gifts of various techniques to reduce stress, such as breathing exercises and visualization. I need your help in dealing with the stress of my work today. I am thankful for the word that comes from you through the Scriptures: "Fear not, for I the Lord am with you wherever you go." Help me to hold onto that promise so that I can be strong in the face of stress in whatever shape it comes today. Amen.

—WDT

A Spiritual Motto

At a stress-filled, deadline-driven time in my life, I discovered an ancient spiritual motto: "Pray and work." Three little words from another time, but they suddenly seemed keenly contemporary. They helped bring sanity to a schedule running out of control. I soon knew I had unearthed a simple prescription for balance amid a harried life. I needed only to carry on in my daily tasks, making sure I did not neglect a deep impulse to turn to God.

When this little motto first began to spread among medieval Europe's monks and spiritual seekers, it was passed along in Latin, with a lilt and rhyme missing in the English: "*Ora et labora.*" St. Benedict, to whom historians trace the genius of the phrase, straddled the fifth and sixth centuries, a time as crowded with stresses and change as ours. Still, Benedict envisioned a life ordered and made rich by both work and prayer. You should get your job done, he said, but not be consumed by it. You should pray, but not to the exclusion of daily responsibilities. As with everything else, work should be given its due, but not more. *Ora et labora.* Pray and work.

—Timothy Jones, *Workday Prayers*

Rejoice in hope, be patient in suffering, persevere in prayer.

—*Romans 12:12*

WORKPLACE PRAYER

O Lord, I remember before you
All the workers of the world;
Workers with hand or brain;
Workers in cities or in fields;
Those who go forth to toil
And those who keep house;
Employers and employees;
Those who command and those who obey;
Those whose work is dangerous;
Those whose work is monotonous and mean;
Those who can find no work to do;
Those whose work is in the service of the poor
Or the healing of the sick
Or the proclaiming of the gospel of Christ
At home or in foreign places. Amen.

—Author unknown

—❦—

*For he is our God,
and we are the people
of his pasture, and the
sheep of his hand. O
that today you would
listen to his voice!*

—*Psalm 95:7*

Being in the Moment

Much has been written about the magical quality of "being in the moment." I believe, however, that this is one of those evergreen bits of wisdom that you can never quite get enough of. As you train your attention to be more focused in this moment, you will notice some remarkable benefits occurring in your work life. You'll be far less stressed out and hurried; more efficient, and easier to be with. You'll also enjoy your work more than ever before, become a much better listener, and will sharpen your learning curve.

—Richard Carlson, *Don't Sweat the Small Stuff at Work*

—❦—

WORKPLACE PRAYER

Gracious God, you know how cluttered my calendar is. You know how little time there seems to be to get everything done that needs to get done. Help me to see this day as your gift and to listen for your voice in it. Deliver me from living in the past, chewing over the "might haves" and the "should haves." Deliver me as well from living too far in the future, dreaming of what may or may not come to pass. Guide me to use the experience of this day's work to inform and energize me to be what you want me to be. Help me to live in each moment by the power of your Spirit and to rejoice in your presence. Amen.

—WDT

Contented Living

Nine requisites for contented living: Health enough to make work a pleasure. Wealth enough to support your needs. Strength to battle with difficulties and overcome them. Grace enough to confess your sins and forsake them. Patience enough to toil until some good is accomplished. Charity enough to see some good in your neighbor. Love enough to move you to be useful and helpful to others. Faith enough to make real the things of God. Hope enough to remove all anxious fears concerning the future.

—Johann von Goethe

WORKPLACE PRAYER

Teacher, I come to you with many questions. I want to be content, but I find myself restless and impatient at times, especially at work. I worry about problems and find it all too easy to be critical. I can't do this on my own. I need you to instruct and guide me. Only you have the strength enough, the patience enough, and the love enough to make contentment possible. I put my life in your guiding hands. Teach me how to be content in you. Amen.

—WDT

I have learned to be content with whatever I have. I know what it is to have little, and I know what it is to have plenty. In any and all circumstances I have learned the secret of being well-fed and of going hungry, of having plenty and of being in need.

—Philippians 4: 11b-12

On-the-Job Prayer

58

The next day Jesus decided to go to Galilee. He found Philip and said to him, "Follow me." Now Philip was from Bethsaida, the city of Andrew and Peter. Philip found Nathanael and said to him, "We have found him about whom Moses in the law and also the prophets wrote, Jesus son of Joseph from Nazareth." Nathanael said to him, "Can anything good come out of Nazareth?" Philip said to him, "Come and see."

—John 1:43-46

Jesus the Worker

Enter the house of Nazareth; approach this workbench where, beside Joseph and under the maternal glance of his mother, the Son of God worked. God-Made-Man knew the experience of human work. We want to enter there, into this house of Nazareth. We want to bring all the modern problems of work: all the social, economic, political, cultural and moral problems, all the anxieties connected with the world of work, especially the worry caused by unemployment. In this house in Nazareth we return close to Jesus the worker. There cannot be human work that is alienated (here). I say this in the name of Jesus. Human work is redeemed, is restored in Jesus Christ.

—Pope John Paul II

WORKPLACE PRAYER

I need your help, O God, to discern your presence in this place of work. It is a long way in time and place from the carpenter shop of Nazareth, but I know that the unseen Jesus is here, just as surely as I am here. Help me today to be aware of his presence. Remind me that I can bring my problems—and all the problems of the world of work—freely to him. Sometimes I am consumed by the tasks at hand, sometimes I am uninterested and bored, and sometimes I am overwhelmed by the pressures on me. Each time, help me to refocus on you. Help me to use the intelligence and experience you have given me to work efficiently and make sound decisions. Keep me close to Jesus the worker, and let me work with the assurance that my work will be redeemed by Jesus Christ. Amen.

—WDT

Willing to Work

We were not idle when we were with you, and we did not eat anyone's bread without paying for it; but with toil and labor we worked night and day, so that we might not burden any of you. This was not because we do not have that right, but in order to give you an example to imitate. For even when we were with you, we gave you this command: Anyone unwilling to work should not eat. For we hear that some of you are living in idleness, mere busybodies, not doing any work. Now such persons we command and exhort in the Lord Jesus Christ to do their work quietly and to earn their own living. Brothers and sisters, do not be weary in doing what is right.

—2 Thessalonians 3:7b-12

―❦―

WORKPLACE PRAYER

Faithful God, I am challenged by Paul's words to the early church. They remind me of my heritage in the membership of the Christian community—of ordinary people who did what it took to carry the gospel where you led them. I am grateful for the example of those who set the standard by working for a living, although they might well have depended on offerings given by the believers. As they persevered through incredible obstacles, so also help me not to be weary in doing what is right—and that includes the work you have given me to do today. Amen.

—WDT

―❦―

We urge you, beloved, to do so more and more, to aspire to live quietly, to mind your own affairs, and to work with your hands, as we directed you, so that you may behave properly toward outsiders and be dependent on no one.

—1 Thessalonians 4: 10b-12

*Let love be genuine…
love one another with
mutual affection;
outdo one another in
showing honor.*

—*Romans 12:9-10*

In Gratitude

A hundred times a day I remind myself
that my inner and outer life depends
on the labors of other men,
        living and dead,
and that I must exert myself in order
to give in the measure as I have received
and am still receiving.

—Albert Einstein

WORKPLACE PRAYER

Giver of Life, receive my thanks for all the gifts you have given me.
Today I especially want to thank you for the gifts of the people
who worked here before I arrived—some long ago and others still
here. I am grateful for their creative ideas that began this work,
for their vision that successfully overcame the challenges, and for
their organization of the systems and procedures that sustain it.
Forgive me for thinking that only I matter in the scheme of things.
And forgive me, equally, for the times when I think I *don't* matter.
Help me to work up to my ability and to serve others with the gifts
you have given me. Help me honor my co-workers today by saying
"thank you." Amen.

—WDT

Simple Justice

How we treat others at work is both a reflection of our spirituality and a contributor to our spiritual development. Virtually no one works completely alone. No matter whether we work in a home, store, office, factory, farm, service or repair facility, church or medical center, courtroom or classroom, plane, train, truck or automobile, work is by its very nature a social endeavor. We all have colleagues, customers, clients, suppliers, competitors, employees, bosses, and fellow commuters. We are all dependent upon others to do our work, and they in turn are dependent on us. So how we deal with others in the workplace — whether that be a paid job or a volunteer activity—is important—not only to the smooth functioning of our economy, but also to our spiritual health, both as individuals and as the human race. The first level of dealing with others at work is simple honesty and justice. We need to know that each worker is going to give "a full day's work for a full day's pay," and that employers pay a just wage and provide decent working conditions. We need to be assured that the products and services we produce and/or purchase are delivered with the best quality possible, at a reasonable price, and without harm to ourselves, others, or our environment.

—Gregory F. A. Pierce, *Finding God@Work*

But let justice roll down like waters, and righteousness like an ever-flowing stream.

—*Amos 5:24*

WORKPLACE PRAYER

Lord, who is an ever-present help in time of trouble, we pray on behalf of all those who work and who hire in our society, asking that you let justice roll down like a mighty stream in the workplace. Let those who are working give an honest day's work and those who are hiring give wages that are fair. And, Lord, if there is injustice anywhere, lend your powerful hand to bring equity into being. We have seen your mighty hand at work and know that you are the same God yesterday, today and tomorrow. In you, O God, we continue to put our trust, and in Jesus' name we pray. Amen.

—*Worship & Daily Life*

Better is little with righteousness than large income with injustice.

—*Proverbs 16:8*

True Righteousness

All one's ways may be pure in one's own eyes,
    but the Lord weighs the spirit.
Commit your work to the Lord,
    and your plans will be established.
The Lord has made everything for its purpose.

—Proverbs 16:2-4

WORKPLACE PRAYER

Holy One, as I reflect on these words of Scripture, I am led to a stronger, deeper reliance on you because this ideal of godliness is frankly beyond me. Like the writer of these Proverbs, my ways may seem right to me, yet only you know what is in my spirit. Only you know who I am at the deepest level and what my motives are. You also know how many challenges there are to godly living in my workplace! By your Spirit, keep me from all forms of injustice and enable me to live in true righteousness today. Amen.

—WDT

Awakening the Corporate Soul

The spiritual dimension can never be amputated from work. It can be ignored but never removed. The words Carl Jung carved over the door of his country retreat, "Called or not called, God is present," remind us that even when we are most oblivious, the spiritual dimension is closer than our breath. In a sense, these words are invisibly carved over the entrance to every company, over every desk and workstation. It is time to pay attention to the most neglected—and the most essential—aspect of our work life. There is, at this time, both a crisis and a longing that permeates organizations across North America. We call one the commitment crisis, the struggle of organizations and their leaders to discover ways to ignite commitment and performance in a rapidly changing, insecure climate. The other is an awakening that is slowly occurring within traditional businesses—the awakening of the Corporate Soul. It is a nascent movement that seeks to reclaim the spiritual impulse that is at the heart of work. It is about people wanting work to have meaning and even more, to engage more of them to the deepest levels of their capacity and desire.

—Eric Klein and John B. Izzo, *Awakening the Corporate Soul*

You have made known to me the ways of life; you will make me full of gladness with your presence.

—*Acts 2:28*

WORKPLACE PRAYER

Breath of Life, you give meaning to every motion I make. You are part of every action, every thought, every feeling. But too often when I arrive at work, I become numb to that. Dear God, infuse me with your sense of aliveness today. Help me to know your presence even in the most mundane moments. I want to serve you, I want to make my work a better place, and I cannot do it alone. Ignite my desire to stay close to you. Fill me with your gladness and use me for your work. Amen.

—WDT

Thus says God, the Lord, who created the heavens and stretched them out, who spread out the earth and what comes from it, who gives breath to the people upon it and spirit to those who walk in it: I am the Lord, I have called you in righteousness, I have taken you by the hand and kept you; I have given you as a covenant to the people, a light to the nations, to open the eyes that are blind, to bring out the prisoners from the dungeon, from the prison those who sit in darkness. I am the Lord, that is my name.

—*Isaiah 42:5-8*

Hope for a Better World

Contrary to a message sometimes prominent in the Christian tradition, incarnational Christians believe work is participation in God's ongoing creation and in Christ's redemption. Good work is a way women and men, individually and collectively, offer their best to the earthly city and to the City of God. Work itself is capable of contributing to the spiritual life. Incarnational Christians are sensitive to inhumane working conditions, unethical business practices, unresponsive social structures, and other blemishes on the plan of God. They are, nonetheless, very optimistic about what is developing in technology, science, industry, construction, commerce, the arts, and other areas of human endeavor. They perceive a strong affinity between openness to the future and Christian hope.

—William Droel, *Full-Time Christians*

WORKPLACE PRAYER

God of the Universe, I am awed that you have taken up residence in me—body and soul. Help me to use the work I do today not just as a means of livelihood but as a way of participating in your work in the world. I grieve for the ways the workplace fails to live up to its possibilities and your vision. I am also glad for the Christians I find who understand that our beliefs and witness in the workplace can change our world. I have to believe, God, that your creative powers are at work in making life better for all of humankind. Thank you for evidence that there is hope for a better world and that the work I do is a part of your plan. Amen.

—WDT

Salt and Light

A positive understanding of work sees the summons of Jesus to be "the salt of the earth" and "the light of the world" as taking expression, first and foremost, in the place where people spend most of their time. Salt preserves and light warns: We have a responsibility to resist evil influences and be alert to moral danger in the workplace. Salt flavours and light guides: We have a responsibility to enhance what is good and witness to Christ. Above all, salt glistens and light shines: We have a responsibility to be true to our nature, authentically, visibly Christian. Jesus does not give us the option of choosing when and where to be salt and light. If salt becomes contaminated, so that it loses its saltiness, or light is perversely hidden, the verdict Jesus gives is unmistakable: It is good for nothing!

—Richard Higginson, *Transforming Leadership*

WORKPLACE PRAYER

Light of the World, you have put me in this workplace to enhance it by my witness to Christ who lives within me. To that end, may I experience the tastiness and the brilliance of the One who is the salt and light of the world. As I work today, help me to resist any defeating negativity I encounter: putting others down, complaining about the boss, laughing at someone else's expense, doing just enough to "get by." Help me to seek what is good and support it, to encourage others who aim to do their best, and to be your visible light in every situation. Amen.

—WDT

You are the salt of the earth; but if salt has lost its taste, how can its saltiness be restored? It is no longer good for anything, but is thrown out and trampled under foot. You are the light of the world. A city built on a hill cannot be hid. Let your light shine before others, so that they may see your good works and give glory to your Father in heaven.

—Matthew 5:13-14, 16

On-the-Job Prayer

66

Do not be conformed to this world, but be transformed by the renewing of your minds, so that you may discern what is the will of God—what is good and acceptable and perfect.

—Romans 12:2

Transformation

If we are sincere in making the request that God's kingdom should come, then we open ourselves up to the possibility that it will indeed be granted, that we may actually be agents of doing God's will. By simple acts of obedient discipleship, we play a part in bringing the present world into closer conformity with that glorious future age of which the biblical passages speak. Situations, not just individuals, can be changed for the better.

In the world of work we may only get occasional glimpses of this. But there are moments worth savouring. Just as there are episodes of awful tedium and depressing futility at work, so there can also be moments of exciting transformation. Examples might include the glow of satisfaction over a finished product, one which has taken a lot of money, time and effort to achieve, but which produces a sense of exhilaration because of the benefits it will bring to those who buy it; the unraveling of manipulative accounting practice, so that confusion and corruption are brushed away and the true state of financial affairs is clearly revealed; or the breakdown of hierarchical structures which have impeded progress, and the establishment of confidence and goodwill between those once dubbed blue and white collar workers.

—Richard Higginson, *Transforming Leadership*

WORKPLACE PRAYER

O Jesus, Master Carpenter of Nazareth, who on the cross through wood and nails did work our whole salvation, wield well your tools in this your workshop, that we who come to you rough hewn may by your hand be fashioned to a more true beauty and a greater usefulness, for the honor of your name. Amen.

—Author unknown

A Higher Purpose

To create a bridge between your spirituality and your work means that you take the essence of who you are and what you believe into your daily work life. You dismantle the dichotomy that so often exists between your spiritual life and that which you do for a living. It means that if kindness, patience, honesty and generosity are spiritual qualities that you believe in, you make every effort to practice those qualities at work. You treat people with kindness and respect. If someone is late or makes a mistake, you try to be patient. Even if it's your job or appropriate to reprimand someone, you do so from a place of love and respect. You are as generous as you can be—with your time, money, ideas and love.

There's something really comforting about creating this spiritual bridge. It reminds you of a higher purpose. It puts your problems and concerns into a broader context. It helps you grow from your difficult experiences rather than become hopeless or overwhelmed by them. It doesn't mean that difficult times become easy—just a little more manageable.

—Richard Carlson, *Don't Sweat the Small Stuff at Work*

I have raised you up for the very purpose of showing my power in you, so that my name may be proclaimed in all the earth.

—Romans 9:17

WORKPLACE PRAYER

Spirit of the Living God, bless the work of my hands, my mind,
   my heart.
May the work offered be a reflection of all that is good within me.
In planning, creating, doing—grant me the courage
   to patiently listen for the stirring of your presence.
Grace me with joyful moments in the midst of daily routine.
Enliven my spirits with humor.
Fill me with reverence for others and gratitude for our diversity.
Nourish my spirit with the awareness that work is holy.
May unity, beauty and truth be the fruit of my labor.
Amen.

—Author unknown

*If there is among
you anyone in need,
a member of your
community in any of
your towns within
the land that the
Lord your God is
giving you, do not be
hard-hearted or tight-
fisted toward your
needy neighbor. You
should rather open
your hand, willingly
lending enough
to meet the need,
whatever it may be.*

—*Deuteronomy
15:7-8*

Serving Others

How often have we passed up an urgent need to minister to the needs of another human being because we don't know what to do or say? What do we say or do when the loved one of a friend or co-worker dies? What do we say or do if that person is in the process of dying? What do we say or do if a couple we have known closely for years begins divorce proceedings? What do we say or do if the child of a friend or co-worker is picked up by the police for pushing drugs? Mostly we do nothing. Yet we all know that our friend or co-worker is hurting and needs consolation and support. Is it God's will that those who are hurting be ministered to? You better believe it. As we go through our daily lives, we need to keep open the way for God to work through us, and we need to be equipped with the skills to be effective priests of the Lord.

—William E. Diehl, *The Monday Connection*

WORKPLACE PRAYER

God of All, I may well meet someone today who is in need. Help me to balance concern for myself with concern for others. Keep me from selfishness. Help me to remember, too, that as I am serving others, I am serving you. When you came in Jesus, you said that whatever I do to others I do to him. When the choice is in doubt, help me to tilt toward others. Assure me that you will look after my interests in ways I cannot know. And for that assurance I am grateful. I come to you with my mind and heart open, with my hands and feet ready to participate in your work of love. Amen.

—WDT

Workaholic Energy

"Workaholics get bad press," says one hard worker who asked to remain anonymous. "The assumption," said the workaholic who owns her own business, "is that all we do is work and that we do it to the exclusion of our family and friends. That's not true." Although she admits she works "all the time" and that her husband also is a workaholic, she says they always make time for each other and their child. "Being a workaholic," she insists, "does not mean you have a psychotic commitment. I take energy I get from work and put it into the rest of my life. It's a nice, big, round circle."

—Carol Kleiman, in *Heigh-Ho, Heigh-Ho*

WORKPLACE PRAYER

Almighty God, eternal measure of all good things,
You fill everything with abundance.
You clothe the lilies of the field and
Feed the young ravens that call on you.
Let your providence be your storehouse,
May the things I need form the basis of what I want.
Never let my wants grow out of greed,
My work to become all-important,
Or my concerns too heavy or distracting.
Help me live in moderation,
Holy, submitted to your will,
Willing to accept whatever you have planned for me. Amen.

—Jeremy Taylor (1613-1667)

On-the-Job Prayer

69

For by the grace given to me I say to everyone among you not to think of yourself more highly than you ought to think, but to think with sober judgment, each according to the measure of faith that God has assigned.

—Romans 12:3

Getting Away from It All

For a growing number of Americans, work is gobbling up not only our time but also our loyalties. Especially for the most well-educated and successfully employed Americans, work identities are overtaking other identities. Work itself is crowding out other life pursuits. Partly because of the personal and portable technologies, partly because of our acquiescence to its claims, work has become an imperial presence—setting up outposts everywhere.

The "getting away from it all" vacation is disappearing as more Americans tote laptops, cellular phones, and portable faxes to the cottage and the beach. Not only is this practice spreading from senior executives to mid- and lower-level managers, but it is establishing a new work norm: never leave the office.

—Barbara Dafoe Whitehead, "Lost in Work,"
The American Enterprise

WORKPLACE PRAYER

God, you are my refuge. You know the pressures of my job. You also know that part of me wants to keep my life in balance. The other part yields too easily to the demands of the workload. When I bring my laptop or paperwork home, or carry home the worries I have about my performance, my co-workers, or the future, I sometimes get out of balance. Help me today to know what is enough. Give me the satisfaction at the end of the day, I pray, that I have done my best. I bring my anxieties to you and ask for the energy and the focus to live and enjoy my life to the full. Amen.

—WDT

The Downside and the Upside

Work can consume our time and energy.
Work can overwhelm our moral code; driven by the dollar.
Work can affect our purity; time without accountability
    both in and out of town.
Work can destroy our marriages; if you're never home,
    should you expect a home to exist?
Work can rip parents away from their children who grow up
    without any role models for life or faith.

However,
Work provides for our daily needs and our life.
Work is what we were created to do; we are made to produce.
Work expands our circle of influence; we can touch the world
    through our work.
Work gives us the opportunity to glorify God in what we do.
Work provides a never-ending stream of opportunities
    to share our faith.
Work is the cultural crossroads where Jesus is most needed.

—The Navigators

WORKPLACE PRAYER

Thank you, God, for the privilege of working. My mind goes to those who have no work and to those who have no hope of working. Whatever faults I find in my job today, whatever complaints I have about the people I work with and for, I am still grateful for the means to earn a living. Forgive me when earning a living is all I see of it, when I take it for granted, or when I complain. Keep me from seeing my work as cumbersome duties or toil. Give me the joy of Christ throughout this day and the opportunity to model him in what I do, and especially in who I am. Amen.

—WDT

The Lord will fulfill his purpose for me; your steadfast love, O Lord, endures forever. Do not forsake the work of your hands.

—Psalm 138:8

Like good stewards of the manifold grace of God, serve one another with whatever gift each of you has received. Whoever speaks must do so as one speaking the very words of God; whoever serves must do so with the strength that God supplies, so that God may be glorified in all things through Jesus Christ. To him belong the glory and the power forever and ever. Amen.

—1 Peter 4:10-11

Work as Ministry

Work itself can be ministry. The word *ministry* comes from the word *service*. Service to others is in itself a ministry. Paul said that everything we do is ministry because we are doing it unto the Lord: "Whatever you do, work at it with all your heart, as working for the Lord, not for men, since you know that you receive an inheritance from the Lord as a reward. It is the Lord Christ you are serving." Work is also worship. *Avodah* is the root word from which we get the words *work* and *worship*. God actually views our work as worship, not as a curse. Eric Liddell, the Olympic gold medal runner who was the star of *Chariots of Fire*, replied remarkably to a challenge from his religious sister. She wanted him to focus on going to the mission field instead of focusing his attention on running. He said, "When I run I feel his pleasure." Eric knew God created him for worship and that worship took many forms.

—Os Hillman, *Faith @ Work*

WORKPLACE PRAYER

Forth in thy name, O Lord, I go,
    My daily labor to pursue,
Thee, only thee resolved to know
    In all I think, or speak, or do.
The task thy wisdom has assigned
    Oh, let me cheerfully fulfill,
In all my works thy presence find,
    And prove thy acceptable will.
Thee may I set at my right hand
    Whose eyes my inmost substance see,
    And labor on at thy command,
    And offer all my works to thee. Amen.

—Charles Wesley (1717-1788)

Work as a Learning Environment

E. F. Schumacher, in his wonderful little book, *Good Work*, suggests that human work has three purposes. It does, of course, provide necessary and useful goods and services. But beyond that, work "enables every one of us to use and thereby perfect our gifts like good stewards (and) to do so in service to, and in cooperation with, others, so as to liberate ourselves from our inborn egocentricity." Written more than twenty years ago, this statement expresses what is now one of the most commonly held transcendent meanings of work. We use our working lives as the anvils on which we hammer out our inconsistencies, hone our skills, and temper our weaknesses. Along with the competencies required by our trades and professions, we learn the fine (and often more difficult) arts of dealing and working with others. Long before 360-degree feedback was in vogue, the workplace was already the arena in which we could learn more about ourselves, if open to doing so, than we could from any other activity. Whether we are struggling to get ahead of the learning curve, or dealing with our petty-tyrant boss, or confronting the terminal illness of a friend and co-worker, work can provide the raw material for our own self-construction.

—C. Michael Thompson, *The Congruent Life*

WORKPLACE PRAYER

Bless to me, O God, everything my eye shall see.
Bless to me, O God, everything my hand shall do.
Bless to me, O God, everything my brain shall think.
Bless to me, O God, the place and the equipment.
Bless to me, O God, the people we shall serve through our work.
Be in the interruptions and the setbacks.
Be in the eye of the person who is difficult.
Be in the eye of the person who is a delight.

—Celtic blessing

On-the-Job Prayer

73

Blessed are the merciful, for they will receive mercy. Blessed are the pure in heart, for they will see God. Blessed are the peacemakers, for they will be called children of God. Blessed are those who are persecuted for righteousness' sake, for theirs is the kingdom of heaven. Blessed are you when people revile you and persecute you and utter all kinds of evil against you falsely on my account. Rejoice and be glad, for your reward is great in heaven.

—Matthew 5:7-12a

For it was you who formed my inward parts; you knit me together in my mother's womb. I praise you, for I am fearfully and wonderfully made. Wonderful are your works; that I know very well.

—*Psalm 139:13-14*

What Defines You?

If pursuit of our work lives has crowded our pursuit of our lives as husbands and wives, mothers and fathers, neighbors, friends, and citizens, does it matter? It may matter a lot. To begin, it makes for a more atomized and disconnected society, where workers jostle and contend in the marketplace, leaving empty chairs at the PTA meetings and volunteer fire departments and church suppers. The result is a weakened and impoverished civil society, a reduced sense of social trust and responsibility, and a decline in the nation's social capital. The incursions of work into family and community life may prove especially detrimental in children. Children are the last American provincials, bound to a particular family and local geography, dependent on the richness and resources of a social world created by adults. That social world is growing more meager and fragile as the work world claims the loyalties and investments of the grownups. From time to time, I read an obituary that describes the recently deceased not as an executive for a pharmaceutical firm or a successful lobbyist, but as a church member or a Red Cross volunteer. Yet it is increasingly difficult to imagine a successful life in these terms—because we cannot imagine ourselves defined by anything but our work.

—Barbara Dafoe Whitehead, "Lost in Work,"
The American Enterprise

WORKPLACE PRAYER

Creator God, I thank you that I am "fearfully and wonderfully made." You have made me a many-sided, complex person, the recipient of multiple talents and capable of far more than I realize. You are the essence of who I am, not my job. When I let my job define me, when I get caught up in my work to the exclusion of everything else, forgive me. Don't let me lose sight of what really matters: devotion to you, love for my friends and family, a balanced life, and a generous spirit. As I work today, help me to do my best to make this workplace a better workplace, the world a better world. Amen.

—WDT

Using Time Well

Use your commute time to pray. On your way to work, pray for people around you on the plane, bus, train or road.

Combine prayer and exercise. If you exercise alone, include conversation with God in the rhythm you establish. Not only will you enhance your prayer life, you will also fill your mind with constructive thoughts while your body is engaged in healthy activity. You will begin to see the results of this regimen in other things you do and in your relationships with your co-workers.

Manage your time. For many people, the secret to success lies in the fact that they know the difference between ten minutes and a quarter of an hour. How many periods of five, ten or fifteen minutes do we waste in the course of a day? Prayer makes optimal use of these transient minutes. God doesn't mind short, more frequent prayers!

Pray for co-workers. When someone's name comes to your mind, pray for that person. Be specific and current when you pray for others. Pray for them not only by name, but also by what you know about the person. Pray about the concerns they express during coffee breaks, at the water fountain, or at lunch.

—*Prayers for the Workplace,* American Baptist National Ministries

Be careful then how you live, not as unwise people but as wise, making the most of the time.

—*Ephesians 5:15-16*

WORKPLACE PRAYER

O Giver of Time, renewed each day with the rising of the sun, I ask for wisdom in how I use the minutes and hours granted to me. May I be generous in using time for acts of compassion and mercy. May I find a rhythm of work, rest, leisure and Sabbath that reflects your will for my life. Daily may my life reflect to others your peace and joy. O Giver of Time, I dedicate my time today to your service. Amen.

—*Worship & Daily Life*

And whatever you do, in word or deed, do everything in the name of the Lord Jesus, giving thanks to God the Father through him.

—Colossians 3:17

Using Your Talents Well

If a man has a talent and cannot use it he has failed. If he has a talent and uses only half of it, he has partly failed. If he has a talent and learns somehow to use the whole of it, he has gloriously succeeded, and won a satisfaction and a triumph few men ever know.

—Thomas Wolfe

WORKPLACE PRAYER

Giver of Life, I am grateful for the abilities you have given me. I am not even sure that I know what all of them are—perhaps some are hidden and yet to be discovered. But I do know that whatever interests and skills I have that enable me to do this job, they come from you. Help me to grow as a person today and to use my talents to the full in the work I do. Keep on revealing to me the places and possibilities where my gifts can make a difference in my workplace and in the wider world. Amen.

—WDT

God's Mission

God cares about workplaces because no part of the world's life has a greater impact—for good or ill—advancing or hindering God's mission—than the decisions made and the dramas acted out in countless workplaces around the globe.

Moreover, God cares about what happens in workplaces because God cares about the individual people who spend a large portion of their lives at work and are shaped significantly by what happens there.

God has a goal for every person. Each of us has been created in the divine image and is intended by God for a future, beginning now and extending beyond this present life, in which we and the whole creation are blessed by God's Spirit, are filled with perfect love, peace, and joy, and are brought into lasting communion with God.

—Paul Minus, *Taking Faith to Work*

WORKPLACE PRAYER

God, I am grateful for my job. Even though you listen to a lot of complaints from me, I know how blessed I am to have work that challenges me and pays the bills. Stir up my creative energies that I might make a worthwhile contribution to this endeavor. May my boss and co-workers experience my support and teamwork. When they look at me, may they see you. Amen.

—Bridget Meehan and Regina M. Oliver, *A Promise of Presence*

On-the-Job Prayer

77

Forgetting what lies behind and straining forward to what lies ahead, I press on toward the goal for the prize of the heavenly call of God in Christ Jesus.

—*Philippians 3:13b-14*

Connecting Faith and Work

Religious communities and our political structures should recognize and encourage a greater connection of faith and everyday life— especially work life. Political debates, at least at the federal level, sadly lack acknowledgement of or attention to the justice gospel. What we do at our jobs and in our community life is every bit as much a part of our faith expression as what we do in more formal religious activities, such as worship service and prayer. Work provides the opportunity for spiritual participation in God's ongoing act of creation. First, work itself is a form of participation in the life of Christ, since all creative effort stems from and reflects God's love. Second, the manner in which work is done—how skillfully, diligently, honestly, effectively, responsibly— reflects ethical values. Third, the social dimensions of work—service to family and community, faithfulness to the work enterprise, collegiality and solidarity with co-workers of all stripes—mark degrees of participation in the mission of the church in the world. Do we, as church, represent Christ in the world of work?

—John Sweeney, AFL-CIO President,
"Dignity in Work as an Article of Faith,"
One Electorate Under God? A Dialogue on Religion and American Politics

*Make every effort
to supplement
your faith with
virtue, and virtue
with knowledge,
and knowledge
with self-control,
and self-control
with steadfastness,
and steadfastness
with godliness,
and godliness with
brotherly affection,
and brotherly
affection with love.*

—2 Peter 1:5-7

WORKPLACE PRAYER

Living God, we come with no great gifts to offer; we are ordinary people. Yet what we have we bring to you, to create new things with you and make your love felt in other people's lives. We offer you our time and our talents at home, at work and in the marketplace. Use us fully so that your love may shine through us, and the light of your kingdom may illuminate the world. Amen.

—*Faith in Business*

A True Calling

A true calling reveals its presence by the enjoyment and sense of renewed energies its practice yields us. This does not mean that sometimes we do not groan inwardly at the weight of the burdens imposed on us or that we never feel reluctance about reentering bloody combat. Facing hard tasks necessarily involves dread. Indeed, there are times when we wish we did not have to face every burden our calling imposes on us. Still, finding ourselves where we are and with the responsibilities we bear, we know it is our duty—part of what we were meant to do—to soldier on.

—Michael Novak, *Business as a Calling*

WORKPLACE PRAYER

Give me, dear Lord, a pure heart and a wise mind, that I may carry out my work according to your will. Save me from all false desires, from pride, greed, envy and anger, and let me accept joyfully every task you set before me. Let me seek to serve the poor, the sad, and those unable to work. Help me to discern honestly my own gifts that I may do the things of which I am capable, and happily and humbly leave the rest to others. Above all, remind me constantly that I have nothing except what you give me, and can do nothing except what you enable me to do.

—Jacob Boehme (1575-1624)

Now as we have many parts in one body, and all the parts do not have the same function, in the same way we who are many are one body in Christ and individually members of one another. According to the grace given to us, we have different gifts: if prophecy, use it according to the standard of faith; if service, in service; if teaching, in teaching; if exhorting, in exhortation; giving, with generosity; leading, with diligence; showing mercy, with cheerfulness.

—Romans 12:4-8

"Real Life"

Too often, we divorce our "work life" from our "real life," from our innermost beliefs and convictions. But "work" can be as much a part of our life—and as much a vehicle for spiritual growth and personal understanding—as going to synagogue or church on Saturday or Sunday or taking a walk in the woods or reading quietly to our kids at bedtime. In fact, work may be among the most potent vehicles for fulfilling our spiritual life because, for many of us, it presents the best opportunities to meld community and social and economic productivity with personal belief and individual talent. To let such an opportunity slip through our fingers is to discard a precious gift.

—Norman Lear, *Being God's Partner*

As for those who in the present age are rich, command them not to be haughty, or to set their hopes on the uncertainty of riches, but rather on God who richly provides us with everything for our enjoyment. They are to do good, to be rich in good works, generous and ready to share, thus storing up for themselves the treasure of a good foundation for the future, so that they may take hold of the life that really is life.

—1 Timothy 6:17-19

WORKPLACE PRAYER

God, I really have no intention of divorcing my work from my faith. But when I think about it, I can see where I have done that, and I ask your forgiveness. By giving me certain skills, and by leading me to this job, you have given me an opportunity to live out my faith. Help me to bring my beliefs through the workplace door today, to the tasks and the relationships I will encounter. Help me to put my faith to work. I am grateful for the opportunity, but I am also in need of your help to make it happen. Amen.

—WDT

Faith at Work

Why the current preoccupation with the meaning of business in America? We don't know for sure. It is probably a combination of factors. One thing we do know: Business people—women and men—are struggling with work and its meaning. At the same time that society is interested in removing alienation from and restoring meaning to business, there have been some profound changes in the Christian view of the marketplace. There has been in the past a strong strain in Christianity separating sanctity from the workaday world. Monkish retreat was not only a discipline reserved for some religious orders. It was suggested as the spiritual model for all Christians, both the laity and the so-called secular clergy. Guard yourself from the temptations of the world, this model said, by imitating the monks in your pieties as closely as possible and by regarding daily life as a distraction or at best a trial to be endured. The new understanding of the Christian message regards the world as a place to discover grace and to bring the good news of the gospel. This new attitude tries to integrate the natural and the supernatural, the this-worldly and the other-worldly.

—William Droel, *The Spirituality of Work*

What good is it, my brothers and sisters, if you say you have faith but do not have works? Can faith save you? Was not our ancestor Abraham justified by works when he offered his son Isaac on the altar? You see that faith was active along with his works, and faith was brought to completion by the works.

—James 2:14, 21-22

WORKPLACE PRAYER

Faithful God, sometimes it is uncomfortable to balance my Christian faith that calls me out of "this world" and my Christian duty to be involved in this needy world. I want my faith to be relevant, and I want my work to be part of my faith. Help me not to lose my balance. Show me how to bring these two callings together. Energize my faith, O God, and help me live an active faith today at my job. Amen.

—WDT

*He was praying in
a certain place, and
after he had finished,
one of his disciples
said to him, "Lord,
teach us to pray."*

—*Luke 11:1*

Prayer at Work

Once, when asked how to pray, a wise spiritual teacher said, "Pick a time, pick a place, and then show up." That advice sounds refreshingly simple. The teacher knew that far more important than the words we use (or stumble over) is a simple decision. Rather than turn prayer into a complicated, out-of-reach regimen, sometimes the important thing is simply to show up, wherever we are, taking advantage of whatever coffee break or lunch hour or commute time we can. We try to still our hearts and minds. And then we turn our thoughts Godward. We let words—our own or those of others—form and guide our devotion.

—Timothy Jones, *Workday Prayers*

WORKPLACE PRAYER

I look to thee in every need, and never look in vain;
I feel thy strong and tender love, and all is well again.
The thought of thee is mightier far than sin and pain and sorrow are.

Discouraged in the work of life, disheartened by its load,
Shamed by its failures or its fears, I sink beside the road.
But let me only think of thee and then new heart springs up in me.

Thy calmness bends serene above, my restlessness to still;
Around me flows thy quickening life, to nerve my faltering will.
Thy presence fills my solitude, thy providence turns all to good.

Enfolded deep in thy dear love, held in thy law, I stand;
Thy hand in all things I behold, and all things in thy hand.
Thou leadest me by unsought ways, and turn my mourning into praise.

—Samuel Longfellow (1819-1892)

The Value of Work

When God finished making the world and the first couple he said, "It is very good." Work has extrinsic value: It is good for what it produces (money, provision for one's family, etc). Work also has intrinsic value: It is good in itself. Mostly, pastoral ministry and people-helping professions are seen as having both intrinsic and extrinsic value while business and the trades are deemed to have only extrinsic value. Are ordinary occupations intrinsically valuable? Making electronic toys, driving a bus, designing a piece of clothing, flying an airplane, teaching in a preschool, working as a hospital nurse?

Certainly those engaged in providing goods or services that seem to have less intrinsic value and durability will require an occupational conversion to view their work as holy, pleasing to God and worthy of God's "it is good." This, of course, is precisely what a good theology of work must do. Where society does not invest meaning in a task, does not socially reinforce it, we must regard this task as God does—as part of making God's world work. Intrinsically work is good for us, good for the world and good for God. This is one of the most crucial and most neglected equipping tasks of the church.

—R. Paul Stevens, *The Other Six Days*

WORKPLACE PRAYER

Almighty God, we bless and praise you that we have wakened to the light of another earthly day; and now we will think of what a day should be. Our days are yours; let them be spent for you. Our days are few; let them be spent with care. Lord, we go to our daily work; help us to take pleasure in it. Show us clearly what our duty is; help us to be faithful in doing it. Let all we do be well done, fit for your eye to see. Give us strength to do, patience to bear; let our courage never fail. When we cannot love our work, let us think of it as your task; and by our true love to you, make unlovely things shine in the light of your great love. Amen.

—George Dawson (1821-1876)

Then God said, "Let us make humankind in our image, according to our likeness; and let them have dominion over the fish of the sea, and over the birds of the air, and over the cattle, and over all the wild animals of the earth, and over every creeping thing that creeps upon the earth." God saw everything that he had made, and indeed, it was very good.

—Genesis 1:26, 31a

*Christ is the image
of the invisible God,
the firstborn of all
creation; for in him
all things in heaven
and on earth were
created, things visible
and invisible, whether
thrones or dominions
or rulers or powers—
all things have been
created through him
and for him. He
himself is before all
things, and in him all
things hold together.*

—Colossians 1:15-17

Integrating Work and Wisdom

The real task I see facing us, as individuals aspiring to live our deepest truth as well as professionals committed to supporting change in the workplace, is to integrate wisdom and work, the spiritual and the practical, to bring the sky to the road and the heart to the marketplace. Can we find the common ground of the bean counter and the dreamer, of those who require measurement, logic and proof, and those who know by intuiting and feeling? Can we merge the drive for productive work and the inner necessity to love and commune with one another? Given the volatile mix of possibilities now interacting unpredictably in our world, it seems essential that we do so. Consciousness does seem to be revealing itself progressively—at least for certain segments of the population—in an emergent holistic and unitive vision of life and work. But are we willing to heal the dualistic split that fragments the person into an object of production and to allow the whole being into our work? Are we willing to integrate our inner and outer lives and see our work as a place of making a meaningful living and encouraging individual fulfillment and freedom? Is leadership enlightened enough to rise to the occasion and recognize the opportunity?

—Let Davidson, *Wisdom at Work*

WORKPLACE PRAYER

O God, I thank you for the great variety of gifts and skills and styles of living that are evident in your creation; for various tasks to do and for various people to be loved; for those in workplaces who count the beans and those who dream the dreams; for the abilities you have given me and the challenges before me. Help me to search my heart and mind for the places I have cut off from you. Heal my brokenness so I can bring my whole being into this day at work. Continually teach me what it means to follow Christ, whose life was the very model of an integrated person. Amen.

—WDT

Ethics in Business

All across our country, there is evidence of a deterioration of ethics. Nowhere is this decline greater than in the world of business. Honest, caring, rational individuals seemingly have come to check their values at the door when they enter the office. The attitude in many businesses appears to be profit at any cost, especially if a company's gains can be at the expense of a competitor—and, sometimes, even if it is at the expense of its customers.

In a competitive business environment where anything goes, ethical considerations have come to be the first to go. Somehow, tough yet simple questions such as "Is this fair?" never get addressed because they are never brought up.... Yet astute business managers know that business success and ethical practices go hand in hand. They have a broader focus on the purpose of business that supersedes daily activities of the business. They know that ultimately there is no right way to do a wrong thing.

—Kenneth H. Blanchard, "Ethics in American Business," *New Traditions in Business*

Let us choose what is right; let us determine among ourselves what is good.

—*Job 34:4*

WORKPLACE PRAYER

Holy One, I sometimes have a hard time deciding what is right and what is wrong. Sometimes it is not at all clear; one way seems as good as another. But I know that people can be affected by my decisions in important ways not always known to me. Give me clarity of thought so that I can measure my decisions by your principles and truths, especially those in the Scriptures that have long guided persons far wiser than I am. Help me see clearly the consequences of my decisions—even those that are unintended. I need your guidance today to choose what is right and good. Amen.

—WDT

*Love does not rejoice
in wrongdoing, but
rejoices in the truth.*

—1 Corinthians 13:6

The "Gray" Areas

Most of us are not faced with major ethical issues in the workplace on a daily basis. If we know something is wrong—and especially if it is also illegal—we simply do not do it. For most of us, in other words, if things are "black and white" we tend to do the right thing. What most of us have to worry about in the workplace are the "gray" areas, the things that are not obviously right or wrong, the decisions that are not clear, the questions that are a little ambiguous. For example, most people struggle with how hard they are supposed to work. Should our nose always be to the grindstone? What, exactly, is "a fair day's work for a fair day's pay"? Is the customer really always right, and if not, how should a customer who is wrong be treated? If the goods or services we are providing people aren't harming them, is that enough? Perhaps our work is not polluting the environment, but are we contributing to the depletion of the world's resources? How do we answer such questions? Many people merely ignore them, but those of us who practice the spirituality of work cannot. For what we seek is integrity, that is, we are trying to achieve a unity or wholeness that allows us to be the same person in all aspects of life—whether we are on the job, at home with our family, or involved in church or community affairs.

—Gregory F. A. Pierce, *Finding God@Work*

WORKPLACE PRAYER

Creator of All that is Good, help me to see today's tasks with your clarity and to do my work with your values. When others cut corners to boost profits, help me to provide full value. When others shade the truth, help me to tell the full truth. When others unthinkingly injure their health by unwise personal decisions, help me to value my body as your gift and care for it with healthy self-love. Teach me when to say something in the face of questionable practices and when to remain silent, that your perfect will may come about. Through Jesus Christ I pray. Amen.

—WDT

Making the Right Decisions

When making a decision of minor importance, I have always found it advantageous to consider all the pros and cons. In vital matters, however, such as the choice of a mate or a profession, the decision should come from the unconscious, from somewhere within ourselves.

—Sigmund Freud

WORKPLACE PRAYER

God of Wisdom, I am sometimes called to make decisions that affect other people. As I strive to weigh the negative and the positive consequences and find the best possible way to go, help me to draw on your wisdom. My ability to make choices is your gift because you created me in your image. As I encounter decisions that need to be made today—great and small—I pray that I may be open to your guidance as you reveal it to me in the depths of my soul. Amen.

—WDT

You are indeed my rock and my fortress; for your name's sake lead me and guide me.

—Psalm 31:3

─────

*Pray without ceasing,
give thanks in all
circumstances; for this
is the will of God in
Christ Jesus for you.*

*—1 Thessalonians
5:17-18*

Finding Time to Pray

The magazine ad for the media company read: "Before deciding on a strategy, developing a plan or negotiating a deal, we indulge in a nearly forgotten ritual: thinking." Has that become true for you? In this cell phone and e-mail driven, Internet-ready world in which we live, can you afford the time to think? Can you afford not to? More importantly, on another level, substitute *praying* for *thinking* in the ad copy. It seems our time has become too precious even to pray. What can you do to counteract the tendency to act first and pray later?

—Bob Peters, in *The Life@Work Journal*

─────

WORKPLACE PRAYER

Patient God, you invite me to come to you. You wait for me; you welcome me. Yet I get caught up so quickly in my to-do lists, meetings, calls, and e-mails at work that I lose sight of you. Help me today to stay in touch with you and to "pray without ceasing" in my thoughts and actions. Thank you that when I do not know how to pray, your Spirit will intercede for me with sighs too deep for words. Thank you for your promise that you are with me always. Amen.

—WDT

Making Sense of it All

"No need is so compelling," wrote the late Willis Harman, "as the need we all feel for our lives to make sense, to have meaning." However dimly conscious it might be amid the chaos and complexity of our daily lives, there is a need in almost all of us for a sense of connectedness and purpose in the events of our outer lives, and a deeply rooted desire for our inner lives to have a harmonious connection to a higher source of meaning and value. Whatever we individually choose to call that source (for me it is God), the reality of the search for it remains the same.

—C. Michael Thompson, *The Congruent Life*

WORKPLACE PRAYER

Gracious God, I lay before you today's chaos. You know all that needs to get done; you know the pressures on me. I bring to you the things that worry me, the things that seem beyond me. I commit to you the hours of this day and ask you to make sense of things that seem disjointed or confusing. Help me to see beyond the day's string of demands to your larger purpose and, most especially, help me to stay rooted in my connection to you. Thank you that you hold me, my day, my job, my co-workers, my workplace, my community—all of us on this chaotic, wonderful planet—in your loving hands. Amen.

—WDT

Commit your work to the Lord, and your plans will be established. The Lord has made everything for its purpose.

—Proverbs 16:3-4a

For the mountains may depart and the hills be removed, but my steadfast love shall not depart from you, and my covenant of peace shall not be removed, says the Lord, who has compassion on you.

—Isaiah 54:10

Serenity

I will try this day to live a simple, sincere and serene life, repelling promptly every thought of discontent, anxiety, discouragement, impurity and self-seeking; cultivating cheerfulness, magnanimity, charity, and the habit of holy silence; exercising economy in expenditure, generosity in giving, carefulness in conversation, diligence in appointed service, fidelity to every trust, and a childlike faith in God.

In particular I will try to be faithful in those habits of prayer, work, study, physical exercise, eating and sleep which I believe the Holy Spirit has shown me to be right. And as I cannot by my own strength do this, nor even with a hope of success attempt it, I look to God my Father, to Jesus my Savior, and ask for the gift of the Holy Spirit.

—Phillips Brooks (1835-1893)

WORKPLACE PRAYER

May there be peace within me today.
May I trust you, God, that I am exactly where you want me to be.
May I not forget the infinite possibilities that are born of faith.
May I use the gifts that I have received.
May I pass on the love that has been given to me.
May I be content knowing that I am your child.
Let your presence settle into my bones.
Allow my soul the freedom to sing and dance and bask in the sun
    of your love.
I am grateful for the work you have given me to do.
Give me your peace in the midst of it all. Amen.

—Author unknown

Offer Yourself

Offer yourself by degrees and as you are able…to worship God, to beg his grace, to offer him your heart from time to time, in the midst of your business, even every moment if you can. Do not always scrupulously confine yourself to certain rules, or particular forms of devotion; but act with a general confidence in God, with love and humility.

—Brother Lawrence

WORKPLACE PRAYER

Lord, make me an instrument of your peace.
Where there is hatred, let me sow love,
Where there is injury, pardon;
Where there is doubt, faith;
Where there is despair, hope;
Where there is darkness, light;
Where there is sadness, joy.
O Divine Master, grant that I may not so much seek
To be consoled, as to console;
To be understood, as to understand;
To be loved, as to love.
For it is in giving that we receive;
It is in pardoning that we are pardoned;
It is in dying that we are born to eternal life.

—St. Francis of Assisi (1182-1226)

I appeal to you therefore, brothers and sisters, by the mercies of God, to present your bodies as a living sacrifice, holy and acceptable to God, which is your spiritual worship.

—*Romans 12:1*

If any want to become my followers, let them deny themselves and take up their cross and follow me. For those who want to save their life will lose it, and those who lose their life for my sake will find it.

—Matthew 16:24b-25

Change Agents for God

God cares passionately about the welfare of all creation. If there is to be constructive change in our world, those of us who see our roles as priests of the Lord need to be the channels of God's acting for the benefit of creation. We need to be change agents for God. Most assuredly, there is a ministry of change and, in one way or another, each Christian can participate in it.

Christians can be faulted far too often for following the first part of the Serenity Prayer, that is, seeking the serenity of accepting things they cannot change. Yet the Bible is filled with stories of God's people in contention with the way things were, in disagreement with commonly accepted practices, and challenging the authority of others. Jesus was such a person. His death was brought about by the religious leaders of his day, who could not tolerate his ministry of change.

—William E. Diehl, *The Monday Connection*

WORKPLACE PRAYER

God grant me the serenity to accept the things I cannot change,
Courage to change the things I can,
And the wisdom to know the difference.
Living one day at a time,
Enjoying one moment at a time,
Accepting hardship as the pathway to peace,
Taking, as he did, this sinful world as it is,
Not as I would have it.
Trusting that he will make all things right
If I surrender to his will.
That I may be reasonably happy in this life,
And supremely happy with him forever in the next.

—Reinhold Niebuhr (1892-1971)

Meeting the Day's Challenges

Taking risks is a creative act. There's something special about letting go of the known that is energizing and exciting. It's scary and exhilarating at the same time. There are no guarantees of success, but our experience has demonstrated time and again that somehow everything works out for the best when you surrender and trust the process. What unfolds is usually surprising and very often filling beyond any expectations you may hold. Follow your passion and be in accord with your gifts—joy is a clue. The challenge of entering unknown territory awakes and enlightens the imaginative flow and enables you to engage whatever you encounter along the way with renewed energy and commitment. It won't always be easy, but the rewards will be singularly surprising.

—Michael and Justine Willis Toms, *True Work*

WORKPLACE PRAYER

Creator God, today is a new day with many unknowns. Old problems may need new solutions. New challenges may call for imaginative solutions. Complex situations may require creative risk-taking. Thank you for your assurance that you are with me, over me, around me, and within me. Wherever I am, and whatever I do, you promise to be my guide and support. I give myself into your hands and entrust this day to you, knowing that you will bless me exceedingly abundantly, above all that I can ask or think. Through Jesus Christ, my companion and strength. Amen.

—WDT

On-the-Job Prayer

93

I am not ashamed, for I know the one in whom I have put my trust, and I am sure that he is able to guard until that day what I have entrusted to him.

—2 Timothy 1:12b

*If we live by the Spirit
let us also be guided
by the Spirit.*

—*Galatians* 5:25

Listening to the Spirit Within

If we do not listen to the Spirit within us, our deepest longings go unfulfilled. Self-doubt and cynicism eclipse confidence and hope…. Technology continues to march ahead, yet chronic social and economic problems get worse. Our national trajectory has failed to solve deepening problems in the workplace. Organizations scramble to downsize and outplace in the hope of avoiding extinction. Businesses lose market share to foreign competitors. Hospitals stagger under spiraling costs, erratic quality, and galloping bureaucracy. Schools are under fire for closing more minds than they open. Frazzled and exhausted managers scratch their heads, often contemplating escape or early retirement.

To recapture spirit, we need to relearn how to lead with soul. How to breathe new zest and buoyancy into life. How to reinvigorate the family as a sanctuary where people can grow, develop, and find love. How to reinfuse the workplace with vigor and elan. Leading with soul returns us to ancient spiritual basics—reclaiming the enduring human capacity that gives our lives passion and purpose.

—Lee G. Bolman and Terrence E. Deal, *Leading With Soul*

WORKPLACE PRAYER

The sacred Three be over me
with my working hands this day
with the people on my way
with the labor and the toil
with the land and with the soil
with the tools that I take
with the things that I make
with the thoughts of my mind
with the sharing of humankind
with the love of my heart
with each one that plays a part
the sacred Three be over me
the blessing of the Trinity.

—Celtic prayer

Holy Work

A few years ago a young taxi driver drove me to John F. Kennedy Airport on Long Island. "So, rabbi," he asked while we sat in heavy traffic, "what do you say to a Jew like me who hasn't been in a synagogue since his bar mitzvah ceremony?"

Thinking a moment, I recalled that in Hasidic lore, the *ball aqalah* (wagon driver) is an honored profession. So I said, "We could talk about your work."

"What does my work have to do with religion?"

"Well, we choose how we look at the world and at life. You're a taxi driver. But you are also a piece of the tissue that connects all humanity. You're taking me to the airport. I'll go to a different city and give a couple of lectures that might touch or help or change someone. I couldn't have gotten there without you. You help make that connection happen. I heard on your two-way radio that after you drop me off, you're going to pick up a woman from the hospital and take her home. That means that you'll be the first non-medical person she encounters after being in a hospital. You will be a small part of her healing process, an agent in her re-entry into the world of health. You may then pick up someone from the train station who has come home from seeing a dying parent. You may take someone to the house of the one that he or she will ask to join in marriage. You're a connector, a bridge builder. You're one of the unseen people who make the world work as well as it does. That is holy work. You may not think of it this way, but yours is a sacred mission."

—Rabbi Jeffrey K. Salkin, *Being God's Partner*

WORKPLACE PRAYER

I pray for those who paint the underside of boats; for makers of ornamental drains on roofs too high to be seen; for cobblers who labor over inner soles; for seamstresses who stitch the wrong side of linings; for dentists who polish each gold surface of the fillings of upper molars; for sewer engineers and those who repair water mains; for electricians; for artists who suppress what does injustice to their visions; for surgeons whose sutures are things of beauty; for those whose work is for your eye only, who labor for your entertainment, or their own, who sleep in peace, knowing that their effects are unknown. Protect them from downheartedness and from diseases of the eye. Grant them perseverance, for the sake of your love which is humble, invisible, and heedless of reward. Amen.

—Mary Gordon, in *Portland Magazine*

On-the-Job Prayer

95

Be holy because I, the Lord your God, am holy.

—*Leviticus 1:2b*

❧

*Do not forsake me
when my strength
is spent…do not be
far from me; O my
God, make haste to
help me! You who
have made me see
many troubles and
calamities will revive
me again; from the
depths of the earth
you will bring me
up again. You will
increase my honor,
and comfort me once
again.*

—*Psalm 71:
9,12,20,21*

"If I Could Change Jobs"

Drudgery days. We all have those days when work seems so dull, we wonder if we really like our jobs any more and why we got into them. Is it all a big mistake? Or has God suddenly changed his mind about where our futures are headed? When life has just seemed to lose its zip, it's time to take a look at where you are. Is it a lack of challenge on this job? Do you need to take more time away from work, perhaps going on a vacation or taking a day off? Lots of things contribute to our drudgery days. But one thing we cannot stop doing—we cannot stop doing good in Jesus' name, on the job or off. No matter what the cause of our drudgery, if we reconnect to God and follow his commands about our situations, he will help us find a way out—one that will not leave us feeling bored and useless. When we stick with it, we will reap an unexpected harvest. God has promised it.

—Pamela McQuade, *Daily Wisdom for the Workplace*

❧

WORKPLACE PRAYER

Provider God, you know that I need this job. You know how important my paycheck is. But you also know that I don't always love my work. You know the things that frustrate me, that make me angry, that add to my weariness. Direct my attention today to what is good about my work. Help me to feel gratitude for the ability to contribute to the output of this place. Keep me from anxiety about my job and the fiction that my work might be better somewhere else. Thank you, God, for all the opportunities and abilities you have given me; help me to utilize them in this workplace today. Amen.

—WDT

Elusive Happiness

For me, happiness came from prayer to a kindly God, faith in a kindly God, love for my fellow man, and doing the very best I could every day of my life. I had looked for happiness in fast living, but it was not there. I tried to find it in money, but it was not there, either. But when I placed myself in tune with what I believe to be fundamental truths of life, when I began to develop my limited ability, to rid my mind of all kinds of tangled thoughts and fill it with zeal and courage and love, when I gave myself a chance by treating myself decently and sensibly, I began to feel the stimulating, warm glow of happiness.

—Edward Young (1683-1765)

WORKPLACE PRAYER

Loving God, happiness seems so elusive. Sometimes I do feel your joy: in my prayers, in my faith, in being in tune with the fundamental truths of life. At other times, it seems that, no matter how hard I try, happiness is elusive. At work today, I place myself in your hands so that I may experience the happiness that comes from knowing my work pleases you. I believe you have put me here, and that when I am at my best both you and I are happy at the highest level. Amen.

—WDT

As the Father has loved me, so I have loved you; abide in my love. If you keep my commandments, you will abide in my love, just as I have kept my Father's commandments and abide in his love. I have said these things to you so that my joy may be in you, and that your joy may be complete.

—John 15:9-11

On the day I called,
you answered me, you
increased my strength
of soul.

—Psalm 138:3

Tending the Soul

Care of the soul requires ongoing attention to every aspect of life. Essentially it is a cultivation of ordinary things in such a way that soul is nurtured and fostered…. Ordinary things have a great deal to do with the condition of the soul. If we do not tend the soul consciously and artfully, then its issues remain largely unconscious, uncultivated, and therefore often problematic.

One of the most unconscious of our daily activities from the perspective of the soul is work and the settings of work—the office, factory, store, studio or home. I have found in my practice over the years that the conditions of work have at least as much to do with disturbances of soul as marriage and family. Yet it is tempting simply to make adjustments in response to problems at work without recognizing the deep issues involved. Certainly we allow the workplace to be dominated by function and efficiency, thereby leaving us open to the complaints of neglected soul. We could benefit psychologically from a heightened consciousness about the poetry of work—its style, tools, timing and environment.

—Thomas Moore, *Care of the Soul*

WORKPLACE PRAYER

God, you are the Great Provider. Forgive me when I come to work without an awareness that my job is your provision for my living. Forgive me when I have not taken time to pray for your guidance that I may do my work in a way that pleases you. Help me today to tend to the needs of my soul in the midst of tending to business. Especially help me to see beyond the mind-numbing details of this day to the larger beauty of my work as a way of serving others. Bring to my awareness the moments of beauty in this work: the surprise connection with another, the satisfaction of helping someone, the pride in a job well done. Let moments of reflection and prayer remind me of your great love for me and your provision for my every need. Through Jesus Christ I offer this prayer and myself. Amen.

—WDT

Abundant Life

Spirituality at work is not first and foremost about achieving our goals, making more money, becoming better managers, finding ways to get others to do what we want, or even about becoming happier, although any and all of these may and do happen when soul-making is taken seriously. What spirituality at work is about is abundant life: living fully into each moment, paying attention to what's happening within us and around us, understanding what our lives are about and how we're meant to make a difference within the larger communities of which we are a part. It is, finally, about our deciding to act, to make creative choices that will move us and our organizations toward a deeper wholeness.

—Whitney Wherrett Roberson, *Life and Livelihood*

WORKPLACE PRAYER

Lord Jesus, as I enter this workplace, I bring your presence with me.
I speak your peace, your grace, and your perfect order into the
    atmosphere of this office.
I acknowledge your lordship over all that will be spoken,
thought, decided and accomplished within these walls.

Lord Jesus, I thank you for the gifts you have deposited in me.
I do not take them lightly, but commit to using them responsibly
    and well.
Give me a fresh supply of truth and beauty on which to draw as I do
    my job.

Anoint my creativity, my ideas, my energy so that even my smallest
    task may bring you honor.
Lord, when I am confused, guide me; when I am weary, energize me.
Lord, when I am burned out, infuse me with the light of your Holy
    Spirit.

May the work that I do and the way I do it bring hope, life and
    courage to all that I come in contact with today.
And O Lord, even in this day's most stressful moment, may I rest in
    you.
In the name of Jesus my Savior I pray. Amen.

—Author unknown

On-the-Job Prayer

99

I came that they may have life, and have it abundantly.

—John 10:10b

The Spirit of Cheerfulness

*If the Lord had not
been my help, my soul
would soon have lived
in the land of silence.
When I thought,
"My foot is slipping,"
your steadfast love,
O Lord, held me up.
When the cares of my
heart are many, your
consolations cheer my
soul.*

—Psalm 94:17-19

Let me but do my work from day to day,
    In field or forest, at the desk or loom,
    In roaring marketplace or tranquil room;
    Let me but find it in my heart to say,
When vagrant wishes beckon me astray,
    "This is my work; my blessing, not my doom;
    Of all who live, I am the one by whom
    This work can best be done in the right way."
Then shall I see it not too great, nor small,
    To suit my spirit and to prove my powers;
    Then shall I cheerful greet the laboring hours,
And cheerful turn, when the long shadows fall
    At eventide to play and love and rest,
    Because I know for me my work is best.

    —Henry van Dyke, "The Three Best Things: (I) Work"

WORKPLACE PRAYER

Giver of Life, I am grateful for the spirit of cheerfulness in this
beautiful poem. I pray for that spirit in myself as I work today
and move through my job's demands. I know from experience that
"vagrant wishes" can distract me both from my work and from the
knowledge that my work is indeed a blessing—to the larger purposes
of this enterprise and to those who are supported by what I earn. I
turn the cares that trouble my heart over to you and ask you to hold
me up. Infuse my work with gratitude and cheer my soul. Amen.

—WDT

Creed for Working Christians

We believe in God, the Creator of this amazing universe, who continues to make all things new. From new galaxies to the birth of a child, from new learning and discoveries in science to the arrival of spring after a difficult winter, God is creating. We believe, O Creator God, that you are constantly weaving the fiber of goodness within the world.

We believe in Jesus Christ, the Savior of this world, who shows the way for living life to its full potential. It is Christ who leads us to seek forgiveness and conveys through his life and death the immense love of God available to all. It is Christ who asks us to have the hearts of little children and to trust and love God wholly and to love our neighbor as ourselves. We believe, O Christ, that you are constantly calling us to be transformed to your likeness.

We believe in the Holy Spirit, the presence of God daily in our lives, the Spirit of truth, justice and love, who guides and informs us, and the comforting attendant who holds us when we are passing through dark valleys. Joy, patience, compassion—all come from the Holy Spirit. We believe, O Spirit of God, that you seek to be present in every dimension of our lives.

O triune God, may we know you fully and may our lives glorify you.

—*Worship & Daily Life*

On-the-Job Prayer

101

I can do all things through him who strengthens me.

—*Philippians 4:13*

WORKPLACE PRAYER

O God,
Creator, Savior and Holy Spirit—
Help me to remember
that nothing
is going to happen
to me today
that you and I
together can't handle. Amen.

—Author unknown

Acknowledgments

I am grateful to friends who contributed some of the reflections and prayers and to a number of volunteers who used this material over a three-month period as a spiritual discipline. They deserve the appreciation of author and readers for their insightful comments that helped to shape this book. I am especially grateful to Marcia Broucek, my editor, who helped me find appropriate Scriptures, refined many of my prayers, tracked down references, and created the helpful subject index.

Resources for Readers

Sources of Reflections

Barrett, Richard. *Liberating the Corporate Soul: Building a Visionary Organization*. Oxford: Butterworth-Heinemann, 1998.

Blanchard, Kenneth. "Ethics in American Business," in *New Traditions in Business: Spirit and Leadership in the 21st Century* (John Renesch, ed). San Francisco: Berrett-Koehler, 1992.

Bolman, Lee G., and Terrence E. Deal, *Leading with Soul: An Uncommon Journey of Spirit*. San Francisco: Jossey-Bass, 2001.

Book of Common Prayer (Episcopal). New York: Church Pension Fund, 1979.

Buechner, Frederick. *Beyond Words: Daily Readings in the ABC's of Faith*. San Francisco: HarperSanFrancisco, 2004.

Carey, George. "Empowering the Priesthood of All Believers." An address delivered at a conference sponsored by Trinity Church, New York, which was convened in Washington, D.C., on September 11, 1992.

Carlson, Richard. *Don't Sweat the Small Stuff at Work*. New York: Hyperion, 1997.

Davidson, Let. *Wisdom at Work: The Awakening of Consciousness in the Workplace*. Burdett, NY: Larson Publications, 1998.

Diehl, William E. *The Monday Connection: On Being an Authentic Christian in a Monday-Friday World*. San Francisco: HarperSanFrancisco, 1991.

Droel, William. *Full-Time Christians: The Real Challenge From Vatican II*. New London, CT: Twenty-Third Publications, 2002.

Droel, William. *Spirituality of Work: Business People*. ACTA and NCL, 1991.

"Economic Justice for All." A pastoral letter on Catholic social teaching and the U.S. Economy written in 1986 by the U.S. Catholic Bishops.

Faith in Business. A quarterly publication of Ridley Hall Foundation, Cambridge, England, and the Industrial Christian Fellowship.

Fox, Matthew. *The Reinvention of Work*. San Francisco: HarperSanFrancisco, 1994.

Gardner, Howard, Mihaly Csikszentmihalyi, and William Damon. *Good Work*. New York: Basic Books, 2001.

Gini, Al, and Terry Sullivan, eds. *Heigh-Ho, Heigh-Ho: Funny, Insightful, Encouraging and Sometimes Painful Quotes About Work*. Skokie, IL: ACTA Publications, 1997.

Halverson, Richard C. *Walk with God Between Sundays*. Grand Rapids, MI: Zondervan, 1982.

Harman, Willis. "Twenty-First Century Business," in *New Traditions in Business: Spirit and Leadership in the Twenty-First Century*. (John Renesch, ed). San Francisco: Berrett-Koehler, 1992.

Hegeman, David Bruce. "The Business of Making Culture," *Business Reform*, Jan/Feb 2002.

Higginson, Richard. *Transforming Leadership: A Christian Approach to Management*. London: Society for Promoting Christian Knowledge (SPCK), 2002.

Hillman, Os. *Faith@Work: What Every Pastor and Church Leader Should Know*. Fairfield, CT: Aslan Publishing, 2004.

Jones, Timothy. *Workday Prayers: On-the-Job Meditations for Tending Your Soul*. Chicago: Loyola Press, 2000.

Klein, Eric, and John B. Izzo. *Awakening the Corporate Soul: Four Paths to Unleash the Power of People at Work*. Canada: Fairwinds Press, 1999.

LayNet. A quarterly publication of The Coalition for Ministry in Daily Life, Emmaus, PA, Fall 2002.

Life@Work Journal, The, Vol 3, No 6, Nov/Dec 2000.

Malone, Richard. *Devotions for Job Seekers: Daily Encouragement Along the Way*. New York: Galilee Trade, 2003.

McQuade, Pamela. *Daily Wisdom for the Workplace*. Uhrichsville, OH: Barbour Books, 2002.

Meilaender, Gilbert C., ed. *Working: Its Meaning and Its Limits*. Notre Dame, IN: University of Notre Dame Press, 2000.

Minus, Paul M. *Taking Faith to Work: Next Steps for Christian Discipleship*. St. Paul, MN: Centered Life, Luther Seminary, 2004.

Moore, Thomas. *Care of the Soul: A Guide for Cultivating Depth and Sacredness in Everyday Life*. New York: HarperPerennial, 1992.

Novak, Michael. *Business as a Calling*. New York: Free Press, 1996.

Pierce, Gregory F. A. *Finding God@Work: Practicing Spirituality in Your Workplace*, Skokie, IL: ACTA Publications, 2004.

Pierce, Gregory F. A. *Spirituality at Work: 10 Ways to Balance Your Life-on-the-Job*. Chicago: Loyola Press, 2001.

Potamkin, Lexie Brockway. *What is Spirit? Messages from the Heart*. Carlsbad, CA: Hay House, 1999.

Prayers for the Workplace. Valley Forge, PA: American Baptist National Ministries.

Prior, David. "Practising God's Presence at Work," Centre for Marketplace Theology Papers #2: *Faith at Work*.

Richmond, Lewis. *Work as a Spiritual Practice*. New York: Broadway, 2000.

Roberson, Whitney Wherrett. *Life and Livelihood: A Handbook for Spirituality at Work*. New York: Morehouse Publishing, 2004.

Salkin, Jeffrey K., and Norman Lear. *Being God's Partner: How to Find the Hidden Link Between Spirituality and Your Work*. Woodstock, VT: Jewish Lights Publishing, 1994.

Sayers, Dorothy L. *Why Work?* An address delivered at Eastbourne, April 23, 1942.

Spitzer, Robert. *The Spirit of Leadership: Optimizing Creativity and Change in Organizations*. Provo, UT: Executive Excellence Publishing, 2000.

Stevens, R. Paul. *The Other Six Days: Vocation, Work, and Ministry in Biblical Perspective*. Grand Rapids, MI: Wm. B. Eerdmans Publishing Company, 2000.

Sweeney, John. "Dignity in Work as an Article of Faith," in *One Electorate Under God? A Dialogue on Religion and American Politics* (E. J. Dionne, Jr., Jean Bethke Elshtain, and Kayla M. Drogosz, eds). Washington DC: Brookings Institution Press, 2004.

Thompson, C. Michael. *The Congruent Life: Following the Inward Path to Fulfilling Work and Inspired Leadership*. San Francisco: Jossey-Bass, 2000.

Toms, Michael, and Justine Willis Toms. *True Work: Doing What You Love and Loving What You Do*. New York: Bell Tower, 1998.

Whitehead, Barbara Dafoe. "Lost in Work," *The American Enterprise*, Sept/Oct 1995.

Whiteman, Thomas, and Randy Peterson. *Stress Test: A Quick Guide to Finding and Improving Your Stress Quotient*. Colorado Springs, CO: Pinon Press, 2000.

Whyte, David. *Crossing the Unknown Sea: Work as a Pilgrimage of Identity*. New York: Riverhead, 2002.

Will, George F. *Men at Work*. New York: Harper Paperbacks, 1991.

Worship & Daily Life: A Resource for Worship Planners (Introduction by Doris Rudy). Nashville, TN: Discipleship Resources, 2002.

Sources of Prayers

(Readers who know the source of any prayers marked "Author unknown" are invited to contact the publisher. Prayers marked "WDT" were written by the author.)

Anderson, Vienna Cobb. *Prayers of Our Hearts in Word and Action*. New York: Crossroad Publishing Company, 1991, p. 45. Used by permission.

Bishop of Ripon, "Faith in Business," in *Work in Worship*, Summer 2000, pp. 17-18. Used by permission.

Book of Common Prayer (Episcopal), New York: Church Pension Fund, 1979, pp. 10, 36, 58, 62, 84, 86.

Byron, Rev. William, SJ, in *Liturgy of the Hours* (Totowa, NJ: Catholic Book Publishing Company, 1999). Used by permission of the author.

Davis, Dawn Elliott. Used by permission.

Gordon, Mary, in *Portland Magazine* (Portland, OR: University of Portland). Used by permission of the author.

McQuade, Pamela. *Daily Wisdom for the Workplace*. Uhrichsville, OH: Barbour Publishing, Inc., 2002, p. 99. Used by permission.

Meehan, Bridget, and Regina M. Oliver. *A Promise of Presence: Weekly Reflections & Daily Prayer Activities*. Skokie, IL: ACTA Publications, 1999, p. 47. Used by permission.

Simpson, Ray, ed., *Celtic Blessings: Prayers for Everyday Life*. Chicago: Loyola Press, 1999. Reprinted with permission of Loyola Press. (To order copies of this book, call 1-800-621-1008 or visit www. loyolabooks.org.)

Worship & Daily Life: A Resource for Worship Planners. Nashville, TN: Discipleship Resources, 1999, pp. 60, 72. Used by permission.

Books of Marketplace Prayers

Adam, David. *Power Lines: Celtic Prayers About Work*. New York: Morehouse Publishing, 1992.

Cooper, Thomas J. *Crossings: Daily Paths from Faith to the Marketplace*. Vancouver: City in Focus Publications, 1999.

Copeland, Germaine. *Prayers That Avail Much for Business*. Tulsa, OK: Harrison House, 2000.

Holton, Bil and Cher. *Business Prayers for Millennium Managers*. Raleigh, NC: Liberty Publishing, 2001.

Jones, Timothy. *Workplace Prayers: On-the-Job Meditations for Tending Your Soul*. Chicago: Loyola Press, 2000.

Kriegbaum, Richard. *Leadership Prayers*. Wheaton, IL: Tyndale House Publishers, 1998.

Malone, Richard. *Devotions for Job Seekers: Daily Encouragement Along the Way*. New York: Galilee Trade, 2003.

McQuade, Pamela. *Daily Wisdom for the Workplace*. Uhrichsville, OH: Barbour Publishing, Inc., 2002.

Websites on Spirituality in the Workplace

Academy of Management—Management, Spirituality & Religion Interest Group: www.aom.pace.edu/msr

ACTA Publications: www.actapublications.com

Association for Spirit at Work: www.spiritatwork.org

Centre for Spirituality at Work: www.spiritualityatwork.org

Christ@Work: www.christatwork.com

Coalition for Ministry in Daily Life: www.dailylifeministry.org

DePree Leadership Center: www.depree.org

Dialogue on Spirituality of Work: www.actapublications.com/spiritwork.html

Episcopal Church USA—The Office for Ministry Development: www.episcopalchurch.org/ministry

Faith@Work: www.faithatwork.com

Faith at Work in Cyberspace: www.actapublications.com/spiritwork.html

Faith at Work New Zealand: www.faithatwork.org.nz

Faith in Daily Life: www.e-spiritu.com/faith.html

Forum for Faith in the Workplace: www.faithintheworkplace.org

Initiatives Newsletter: www.catholiclabor.org/NCL.htm

International Coalition of Workplace Ministries: www.icwm.net

Intervarsity Ministry in Daily Life: www.ivmdl.org

The High Calling of Our Daily Work: www.thehighcalling.org

London Institute for Contemporary Christianity: www.licc.org.uk

Mennonite Economic Development Associates: www.meda.org

National Center for the Laity: www.catholiclabor.org/NCL.htm

Religion & Ethics Newsweekly: www.thirteen.org/religionandethics

Seeing Things Whole: www.seeingthingswhole.org

Spirit in Business: www.spiritinbusiness.org

Spirituality at Work: www.spiritualityatwork.com

The Spirited Workplace: www.spiritedworkplace.com

WorkMatters™: www.workmatters.org

Workplace Spirituality: www.workplacespirituality.info

Yale Center for Faith and Culture: www.yale.edu/faith

SCRUPLES: www.scruples.net

Source Index

Scripture Index

Subject Index

Other Resources on Prayer and Work

Running into the Arms of God: Stories of Prayer/Prayer as Story. Father Patrick Hannon, CSC, uses the liturgical hours as a frame on which to hang twenty-one stories of prayer in the ordinary events of daily life. 128-page hardcover, $15.95; paperback, $11.95

Henri Nouwen Illuminated. Graphic artist Len Sroka combines wisdom from Henri Nouwen's books with photo images to bring new light to the spiritual master's words. 160-page hardcover gift book, $14.95

Prayers from Around the World and Across the Ages. Victor Parachin has compiled a wealth of sublime, reverent and poignant prayers from many of the world's great spiritual traditions. Each prayer is preceded by a one-paragraph biography of the person who composed it. 160-page paperback, $9.95

Spirituality at Work: Ten Ways to Balance Your Life On-the-Job. Gregory Pierce offers ten "disciplines" that can be practiced in virtually every workplace to raise your awareness of the presence of God and to allow that awareness to change how you do your work. 160-page paperback, $14.95

Music to Heal the Body and the Soul. Sheldon Cohen conducts members of the Pacific Pops Orchestra in a reverent, peaceful, inspiring performance of both classical and religious music that is suitable for the workplace. 81-minute double compact disc, $14.95

Praying the New Testament as Psalms. Desmond O'Donnell and Maureen Mohen present a unique new way to experience the riches of the New Testament. Verses from the Gospels, Letters, Acts, and Book of Revelation are used as the basis for 100 original prayers, each arranged in a psalm-like format. 216-page paperback, $12.95

Available from Booksellers or call 800-397-2282
www.actapublications.com